Jean-Pierre de Caussade

the

SACREDNESS

of the

MOMENT

Abandonment to Divine Providence

ш
WHITAKER
HOUSE

Publisher's note: This edition from Whitaker House was adapted from *Abandonment; or, Absolute Surrender to Divine Providence*, edited by Rev. H. Ramière, S.J., and translated from the eighth French edition by Miss Ella McMahon. It was originally published in 1887 by Benziner Brothers, R. Washbourne, and M.H. Gill & Son, New York. Public domain. This new edition has been updated for the modern reader. Words, expressions, and sentence structure have been lightly revised for clarity and readability.

Unless otherwise indicated, all Scripture quotations are taken from the *King James Version Easy Read Bible*, KJVER™, © 2001, 2007, 2010, 2015, 2023 by Global Evangelism, Inc. Used by permission. All rights reserved. Scripture quotations marked (DRA) are taken from the Douay-Rheims 1899 American Edition. Public domain.

THE SACREDNESS OF THE MOMENT:
Abandonment to Divine Providence

ISBN: 979-8-88769-490-0
eBook ISBN: 979-8-88769-491-7
Printed in the United States of America
© 2026 by Whitaker House

Whitaker House
1030 Hunt Valley Circle
New Kensington, PA 15068
www.whitakerhouse.com

Library of Congress Control Number: 2025943784

1 2 3 4 5 6 7 8 9 10 11 ⨺ 33 32 31 30 29 28 27 26

CONTENTS

BOOK ONE

Of the Nature and Excellence of the Virtue of Holy Abandonment

BOOK TWO

*The Divine Action and the Manner in Which It Unceasingly Works
the Sanctification of Souls*

BOOK THREE

*The Paternal Care with Which God Surrounds Souls
Wholly Abandoned to Him*

BOOK ONE

OF THE NATURE AND EXCELLENCE OF THE VIRTUE OF HOLY ABANDONMENT

CHAPTER ONE

SIMPLE AND ABSOLUTE SELF-ABANDONMENT

The sanctity of the righteous under the old law, and of Joseph and of Mary herself, consisted in fidelity to the order of God.

God speaks today as He spoke to our fathers, when spiritual directors were not as numerous or methods of direction as well-defined. All their spirituality consisted in simple fidelity to the order of God; but it was not reduced to a science that explained it so sublimely or minutely, or contained so many precepts, so many maxims, so much instruction. Our present wants, no doubt, require this explanation. It was not so in the first ages of the church, when men were simpler and more upright. Each moment brought a duty to be faithfully fulfilled. This was sufficient for interior souls of that day. Their whole attention was concentrated simply upon the duty of each successive moment with the fidelity of the hour hand of a clock that steadily traverses stroke by stroke the circle in which it is appointed to move. The mind, unceasingly moved by divine grace, turned imperceptibly to the new duty that presented itself in the order of God every hour.

Such were the hidden springs of Mary's life, the most perfect example of simple and absolute self-abandonment to the will of God. The simple words *"Fiat mihi secundum verbum tuum,"*[1] with which she was content to answer the angel, expressed all the mystic theology of the ancients. Then, as now, it was all reduced to the simplest and most absolute abandonment of the soul to the will of God under whatever form it manifested itself. This noble and exalted disposition, the basis of all Mary's spirituality, is brilliantly manifested in the words *"Fiat mihi."* Observe how perfectly they accord with those that our Lord would have ever on our lips and in our hearts: *"Fiat voluntas tua."*[2]

True, the duty required of Mary at that supreme moment was a glorious one for her. But all the splendor of that glory would have made no impression upon her if the divine will, alone capable of influencing her, had not arrested her attention. It was this divine will that guided her in everything. Her occupations, whether ordinary or exalted, were in her eyes but shadows, more or less obscure, in which she found equal means of glorifying God and recognizing the workings of the Almighty. She joyfully accepted the duty or suffering of each moment as a gift from Him who fills with good things the hearts that are nourished by Him alone and not by appearances or created things.

---

1. Editor's note: In several places throughout this work, Caussade employs phrases and sentences from the Vulgate, a Latin translation of the Bible from the late fourth century and early fifth century used by the Roman Catholic Church. English translations of these phrases and sentences, which were retained in Latin by the original translator of this work, are included in the footnotes. Unless otherwise indicated, all translations are either modernized renderings of, or exact quotes from, the Douay-Rheims 1899 American Edition (DRA), an English translation of the Vulgate by members of the Catholic seminary English College in Douai, France. Public domain. *"Fiat mihi secundum verbum tuum"* may be rendered in English as "Let it be done to me according to Your word." (See Luke 1:38.)
2. "Your will be done." (See Matthew 6:10; 26:42.)

CHAPTER TWO

SACRED MOMENTS

*The duties of each moment are the shadows that
veil the divine action.*

"The power of the Highest shall overshadow you,"[3] the angel said to
Mary. This shadow, behind which the power of God effects the
entrance and growth of Jesus Christ in our souls, is the form
assumed by the duties, attractions, and crosses of each moment.

They are in truth but shadows like those to which we give the
name in the order of nature, and which envelop sensible objects
and hide them from our view. Thus, in the moral and supernatural
order, the duties of each moment under their obscure appearances
conceal the truth of the divine will, which alone merits our attention. Thus Mary regarded them. Therefore, these shadows, passing

---

3. Luke 1:35.

before her senses, so far from deceiving her, filled her with faith in Him who is always the same. Withdraw, archangel; your moment passes; you vanish. Mary passes beyond you; she is ever in advance. But the Holy Spirit, with whom she has been filled through the sensible appearances of your mission, will never abandon her.

There are few extraordinary events in the exterior life of Mary. At least, it is not to these that Holy Scripture calls our attention. Her exterior life is represented as very simple, very ordinary. She did and suffered as did others of her condition. She goes to visit her cousin Elizabeth; the other relatives go also. She retires to a stable; it is a consequence of her poverty. She returns to Nazareth; the persecution of Herod had driven her forth. Jesus and Joseph lived there with her by the labor of their hands.

Behold the daily bread of the holy family! But with what bread was the faith of Mary and Joseph nourished? What was the sacrament of all their sacred moments? What did they discover under the ordinary appearance of the events that filled their lives? Exteriorly, nothing more than was happening to the rest of mankind. Interiorly, faith discovers and develops nothing less than God working great things. O bread of angels! Heavenly manna! Pearl of the gospel! Sacrament of the present moment! You give God under appearances as poor and mean as the manger, the hay, and the straw! But to whom do you give Him? *"Esurientes reples bonis."*[4] God reveals Himself to the humble in little things; and the proud, regarding only the exterior, do not find Him even in great things.

---

4. Caussade here adapts a verse from the Vulgate. This sentence may be translated as "You fill the hungry with good things." The Vulgate literally reads, *"Esurientes implevit bonis,"* meaning "He has filled the hungry with good things." (See Luke 1:53.)

CHAPTER THREE

THE COOPERATION GOD REQUIRES

How much easier sanctity becomes when studied from this point of view.

If the work of our salvation offers obstacles that are apparently insurmountable, it is because we do not have a just idea of it. In truth, sanctity consists in but one thing: fidelity to the order of God. This fidelity is equally within the reach of all, whether in its active or in its passive part.

The active part of fidelity consists in fulfilling the duties imposed upon us either by the general commands of God and the church or by the particular state we have embraced. Its passive part consists in lovingly accepting all that God sends to us in each moment.

Which of these two parts of sanctity is above our strength? Not the active part, since the duties it enjoins cease to be duties for us the moment our strength is really unequal to them. Will the state of your health not permit you to hear Mass? You are no longer obliged to do so. And so it is with all positive obligations that prescribe duties to be fulfilled. Only those precepts that forbid things evil in themselves admit of no exception, for it is never permitted to do evil.

Is there anything easier or more reasonable? What excuse can be urged against it? Yet this is all the cooperation God requires of the soul in the work of its sanctification. He requires it of great and small, of strong and weak; in a word, of all, at all times, in all places. Therefore, He requires of us only what is easy, since to attain eminent sanctity requires but a simple goodwill.

If, over and above the commandments, He shows us the counsels as the more perfect end of our efforts, He is ever careful to accommodate their observance to our position and character. As the chief mark of our vocation for the counsels, He sends to us the attractions and graces that facilitate the practice of them. He urges no one but in proportion to his strength and according to his attainments. Again, I ask, what could be more just?

O you who aspire to perfection and are tempted to discouragement by what you read in the lives of the saints and find prescribed in certain pious books! O you who are overwhelmed by the terrible ideas that you form of perfection! It is for your consolation that God permits that I write this.

Learn what you seem not to know.

In the order of nature, the God of all goodness has made necessary things—such as air, water, and earth—common and easy to attain. Nothing is more necessary than breath, sleep, and food, and nothing is more common. Love and fidelity are no less necessary in the spiritual order; therefore, the difficulty of acquiring them cannot be as great as you represent it to yourselves.

Observe your life: Of what does it consist? Of a multitude of unimportant actions. Yet with these same unimportant actions, God deigns to be content. This is the cooperation required of the soul in the work of its perfection. God Himself expresses it too clearly for there to be any doubt about it: *"Fear God, and keep His commandments: for this is the whole duty of man."*[5] That is to say, this is all that is required on man's part; in this consists his active fidelity. Let him fulfill his part; God will do the rest. Grace, working by itself, effects marvels that surpass the intelligence of man. For ear has not heard, eye has not seen, and heart has not felt what God conceives in His mind, resolves in His will, and executes by His power in souls wholly abandoned to Him.

The passive part of sanctity is still easier, since it consists in accepting what, very often, we cannot avoid, and in bearing with love—that is, with consolation and sweetness—what we too frequently endure with weariness and irritation. Again let me repeat: herein lies all sanctity. It is the grain of mustard seed whose fruits we do not gather because we fail to recognize it in its littleness. It is the drachma of the gospel, the treasure that we do not find, do not seek, because we imagine it to be too far beyond us.

Do not ask me the secret of finding this treasure, for there is no secret. This treasure is everywhere; it is offered to all, at all times, in all places.

Through creatures, friends, and enemies, it flows plentifully; it flows over the faculties of our bodies, of our souls, and into the very center of our hearts. Let us but open our mouths, and they will be filled. The divine action floods the universe: it penetrates all creatures; it floats above them, about them; it is ever present with

---

5. Ecclesiastes 12:13.

them; it precedes them; it accompanies them; it follows them; and they have but to allow themselves to be borne onward on its tide.

If kings and their ministers, princes of the church and of the world, priests, soldiers, peasants, laborers—in a word, all men—only knew how easily they can attain eminent sanctity! They have but to fulfill the simple duties of religion and their state in life, and to bear with submission the crosses these duties bring, and to accept with faith and love the work and suffering that, unsought and unceasingly, come to them through the order of Providence. This is the spirituality that sanctified the patriarchs and prophets before there were so many methods and so many masters in the spiritual life.

This is the spirituality of all ages and of all states, which cannot be more surely sanctified, or be in a manner more noble, more extraordinary, more easy, than by the simple use of that which God, the Sovereign Director of souls, gives to them each moment to do or to suffer.

CHAPTER FOUR

LIVING AND ACTING BY THE ORDER OF GOD

Perfection does not consist in knowing the order of God but in submitting to it.

The order of God, the good pleasure of God, the will of God, the action of God, the grace of God—all these are one and the same thing in this life. It is God's laboring to render the soul like unto Him. Perfection is nothing but the soul's faithful cooperation in this labor of God. This work is silently effected in our souls, where it thrives, increases, and is consummated unconsciously to ourselves.

Theology is full of conceptions and expressions that explain the wonders of this work effected in individual souls according to their capacity. We may know all the theory of this work, admirably write and speak about it, and instruct and direct souls. Yet if our knowledge is only theoretical, then I say that in comparison with souls who live and act by the order of God and are guided by His divine will, though they are ignorant of the theory of its operations or its different effects and are unable to speak of them, we are like a sick physician compared to ordinary people in perfect health.

The order of God, His divine will, received with simplicity by a faithful soul, effects this divine work in her unconsciously to herself, just as a medicine submissively taken restores the health of a sick man, although he does not have, and does not need to have, any knowledge of medicine.

It is the fire that warms us—not the philosophical knowledge of the element and its effects. So it is the order of God, His divine will, and not the curious speculation on its principles and its methods, that produces the sanctification of our souls.

If we thirst, we must drink; theoretical explanations will not quench our thirst. Curiosity for knowledge only makes us thirst still more. Therefore, if we thirst for sanctification, curious speculations only keep us further from it. We must abandon all theories and drink in simplicity of all that the will of God sends us of work and suffering.

That which comes to us each moment by the order of God is best and holiest and most divine for us.

CHAPTER FIVE

THE FULLNESS OF ALL OUR MOMENTS

Reading and other exercises sanctify us only insofar as they are the channels of the divine action.

All our science consists in recognizing God's will in regard to the present moment. All reading pursued in any spirit other than that of submission to the order of God is injurious. The will of God, the order of God, is the grace that works in the depths of our hearts by means of our readings and by all our other works. Without it, our readings are but shadows, vain appearances, which, coming to us devoid of the vivifying virtue of the order of God, serve only to empty the heart by the very fullness they cause in the mind.

The virtue of this divine will flowing into the soul of a simple, ignorant girl, by means of suffering or ordinary actions, effects in the depths of her heart this mysterious work of the supernatural Being without filling her mind with any idea likely to awaken pride, whereas the proud man who studies spiritual books only through curiosity and does not unite his reading to the will of God receives into his mind the letter without the spirit and becomes colder and more hardened than ever.[6]

The order of God, His divine will, is the life of the soul under whatever appearances the soul receives it or applies it to herself.

Whatever may be the relation of the divine will to the mind, it nourishes the soul and unceasingly strengthens her growth by giving her, each moment, what is best for her. Nor is one thing more efficacious than another in producing these happy effects; no, it is simply the duty of the present moment that comes to us by the order of God. That which was best for us in the past moment is no longer best for us, for it is stripped of the will of God, which has passed on to other things from which it creates for us the duty of the present moment. And it is this duty, under whatever appearance it is manifested, which will now most perfectly sanctify our souls.

If the divine will makes reading the duty of the present moment, the reading will effect His mysterious work in the depths of the soul. If, in obedience to the divine will, we leave the reading for the duty of contemplation, this duty will create the new man in the depths of the heart, and reading would then be injurious and useless. If the divine will withdraws us from contemplation to hear confessions or to perform other duties, and that during a considerable time, these duties will form Jesus Christ in the depths of the heart, and all the sweetness of contemplation would only serve to banish Him.

The order of God is the fullness of all our moments. It flows under a thousand different appearances that, successively becoming

---

6. See 2 Corinthians 3:6.

our present duty, form, increase, and complete the new man in us, in all the fullness that the divine wisdom has destined for us. This mysterious growth of Jesus Christ in us is the work produced by the order of God; it is the fruit of His grace and of His divine will. This fruit, as we have said, is germinated, increased, and nourished by the succession of our present duties filled with the virtue of this same divine will.

In fulfilling these duties, we are always sure of possessing the "better part,"[7] for this holy will is itself the better part. We have but to yield to it, to blindly abandon ourselves to it with perfect confidence. It is infinitely holy, infinitely wise, infinitely powerful for souls who unreservedly hope in it, who love and seek but it alone, and who believe with unfaltering faith that what it assigns to each moment is best without seeking elsewhere for more or less, and without pausing to consider the relation of material things with the order of God, which is the seeking of pure self-love.

The will of God is the essential, the reality and virtue, of all things. It is that which adapts and renders them suitable to the soul. Without it, all is emptiness, nothingness, falsehood, the empty husk, the letter without the spirit, vanity, death.

The will of God is the health, the life, the salvation of soul and body, whatever its manifestations or ways of reaching us. Therefore, we must not judge the virtue of things by the relations they bear to mind or body, for these relations are unimportant. It is the will of God alone that gives to all things, whatever they may be, the power to form Jesus Christ in the depth of our hearts. We must frame no laws for this will and place no limit to its action, for it is all-powerful.

Whatever the ideas that fill the mind, whatever the feelings that the body experiences, if it were for the mind but distractions and trouble, for the body but sickness and death, the divine will

---

7. See Luke 10:42.

nevertheless is ever, for the present moment, the life of body and soul. For both one and the other, whatever their condition, are sustained by it alone. Without it, bread is poison; and, through it, poison becomes a salutary remedy. Without it, books only confuse and trouble us; with it, darkness is turned into light. It is the wisdom, the truth, of all things. In all things, it gives us God—and God is the infinite Being who holds the place of all things to the soul who possesses Him.

CHAPTER SIX

SEEING GOD ALONE IN ALL THINGS

The mind and other human means are useful only insofar as they are the instruments of the divine action.

The mind, with all its powers, would hold the first place among the instruments of the divine will; but it must, like a dangerous slave, be reduced to the last. The simple of heart who know how to use it can derive great profit from it; but it can also do much injury when not kept in subjection.

When the soul sighs after created means, the divine action whispers to the heart that it suffices. When she would injudiciously reject them, the divine action whispers that they are instruments not to be taken or rejected at will but to be simply received from Providence and adapted to the order of God—the soul thus using all things as though not using them, being deprived of all things yet lacking nothing.

The divine action, being limitless in its fullness, can take possession of a soul only insofar as the soul is void of all confidence in her own action; for this confidence and self-activity fill the heart to the exclusion of the divine action. It is an obstacle that, existing in the soul herself, is more likely to arrest the divine action than exterior obstacles, which Providence can change at will into powerful aids. For it can work with all things, even those that are in themselves useless. With the divine will, nothing is everything, and, without it, everything is nothing.

Whatever the value in itself of meditation; contemplation; vocal prayer; interior silence; acts of the will, whether sensible, distinct, or less perceptible; retreat; or active life—better than all of these is what God wills for the soul at the present moment, and the soul should regard everything else with perfect indifference, as being of no value whatever.

Thus, seeing God alone in all things, she should take or leave them at His pleasure in order to live in, hope in, and be nourished by Him and not by the things that have force and virtue only through Him. Under all circumstances, the soul should constantly say with St. Paul, *"Lord, what will You have me to do?"*[8] Not this more than that, but simply Your will—so worthy of adoration! The spirit loves one thing, the flesh another;[9] but, Lord, let Your will be mine. Contemplation; action; prayer, vocal or mental, affective or passive; light or darkness; special or general graces—all these are nothing, Lord, for in Your will lies their sole virtue. Your will alone is the end of all my devotion, and not these things, however elevated or sublime in themselves, for the end of divine grace is the perfection of the heart, not of the mind.

---

8. Acts 9:6.
9. See Matthew 26:41; Mark 14:38.

The presence of God that sanctifies our souls is that indwelling of the Trinity that penetrates to the depths of our hearts when they are submissive to the divine will. For the presence of God that we enjoy through the exercise of contemplation effects this intimate union in us only as do all other things that come to us in the order of God. It holds, however, the first rank among them, for it is the most excellent means of uniting oneself with God when He wills that we should use it.

We may therefore justly esteem and love contemplation and other pious exercises, provided the foundation of this esteem and love is wholly God, who mercifully deigns through them to communicate Himself to our souls.

We receive the prince himself when we receive his suite. It would be showing him little respect to neglect his officers under the pretext of possessing him alone.

CHAPTER SEVEN

WHY SEEK
IT ELSEWHERE?

There is no enduring peace but in submission to the divine action.

The soul who is not united solely to the will of God will find neither rest nor sanctification in any self-chosen means—not even in the most excellent exercises of piety. If what God Himself chooses for you does not suffice, what other hand can minister to your desires? If you turn from the food that the divine will itself has prepared for you, what choice foods will not prove insipid to a taste so depraved? A soul cannot be truly nourished, strengthened, purified, enriched, and sanctified except by the fullness of the present moment. Then what more would you have? Since you here find all good, why seek it elsewhere? Are you wiser than God? Since He ordains that it should be thus, how could you desire that it should be otherwise? Can His wisdom and goodness err? Should you not from the moment He ordains an event be utterly convinced that it is the best that could happen? Do you think you will find peace in struggling with the Almighty? On the contrary, is it not this struggle too often renewed, almost unconsciously, that is the cause of all our disquiet? It is but just that the soul who is not satisfied with the divine fullness of the present moment should be punished by an inability to find contentment in anything else.

If books, the example of the saints, and spiritual discourses destroy the peace of the soul, if they fill without satisfying, it is a mark that we have not received them in simple abandonment to the divine action but have taken them ourselves in a spirit of proprietorship. Their fullness, therefore, bars the entrance of God to the soul, and we must rid ourselves of it as an obstacle to grace. But when the divine action ordains the use of these means, the soul receives them as it does everything else—that is, in the order of God. She accepts them as she finds them, in her fidelity simply using them, never appropriating them; and, their moment passed, she abandons them to find her contentment in what follows in the order of Providence. In truth, there is nothing really beneficial for me but that which comes to me in the order of God. Nowhere can I find any means, however good in itself, more efficacious for my sanctification and more capable of giving peace to my soul.

CHAPTER EIGHT

GOD'S GOOD PLEASURE

*The perfection of souls and the excellence of different states are in
proportion to their conformity to the order of God.*

The order of God gives to all things that concern the faithful
soul a supernatural and divine value. All that it exacts, all that it
embraces, and all the objects upon which it sheds its light become
holiness and perfection, for its virtue is limitless: it makes all that
it touches divine. But in order to keep ourselves in the path of perfection, swerving neither to the right nor to the left, the soul must
follow no inspiration that she assumes comes from God without
first assuring herself that it does not interfere with the duties of
her state in life. These duties are the most certain indications of the
will of God, and nothing should be preferred to them. In fulfilling
them, there is nothing to be feared, no exclusion or discrimination

to be made. The moments devoted to them are the most precious and salutary for the soul from the fact that she is sure of accomplishing the good pleasure of God.

All the perfection of the saints consists in their fidelity to the order of God; therefore, we must refuse nothing, seek nothing, but accept all from His hand, and nothing without Him. If they come to us in the order of God, then books, wise counsels, vocal prayers, and interior affections instruct, guide, and unite the soul to Him. Quietism errs when it disclaims these means and all sensible appearances, for there are souls whom God wills shall always be led in this way, and their state and their attractions clearly indicate it. In vain we picture to ourselves methods of abandonment from which all action is excluded. When the order of God causes us to act, our sanctification lies in action.

Besides the duties of each one's state, God may further ask certain actions that are not included in these duties, though not contrary to them. Attraction and inspiration, then, indicate the divine order. And the most perfect for souls whom God leads in this way is to add things inspired to things of precept, but always with the precautions that inspiration requires to prevent its interfering with the duties of one's state and the ordinary events of Providence.

God makes saints as He chooses. They are formed by His divine action, to which they are ever submissive, and this submission is the truest abandonment and the most perfect.

Fidelity to the duties of one's state and submission to the dispositions of Providence are common to all the saints. They live hidden in obscurity, for the world is so fatal to holiness that they would avoid its quicksands. Yet their sanctity does not consist in this but wholly in their entire submission to the order of God. The more absolute their submission, the greater their sanctity. We must not imagine that those whose virtues God is pleased to brilliantly manifest by singular and extraordinary works, by undoubted attractions and inspirations, are any less faithful in the path of abandonment. Once the order of God makes these brilliant works a duty, if they content themselves with the duties of their state and the ordinary events of Providence, they fail in abandonment to Him and His will, which ceases to rule their every moment, and their every moment ceases to be the exponent of the will of God. They must study and measure their efforts according to the standard of God's designs for them in that path that their attractions indicate to them. Fidelity to inspiration is for them a duty. As there are souls whose whole duty is marked by an exterior law and who must be guided by it because God confines them to it, so also there are others who, besides their exterior duties, must be further faithful to that interior law that the Holy Spirit engraves upon their hearts.

But who are the most perfect? Vain and idle research! Each one must follow the path that is traced for him. Perfection consists in absolute submission to the order of God and carefully availing ourselves of all that is most perfect in it. It advances us little to weigh the advantages of the different states considered in themselves, since it is neither in the quality nor quantity of things enjoined that sanctity is to be sought. If self-love is the principle of our actions, or if we do not correct it when we recognize its workings, we will always be poor in the midst of an abundance not provided by the order of God. However, to decide the question to some extent, I think that sanctity corresponds to the love one has for God's good pleasure, and the greater one's love for this holy will and this order, whatever the character of their manifestations, the greater one's sanctity. This is manifest in Jesus, Mary, and Joseph, for, in their private life, there is more of love than of grandeur, and more of spirit than of matter. And it is not written that these sacred persons sought the holiest of things but holiness in all things.

We must therefore conclude that there is no special way that can be called the most perfect, but that the most perfect in general is fidelity to the order of God, whether in the accomplishment of exterior duties or in the interior dispositions, each one according to his state and calling.

I believe that if souls seriously aspiring to perfection understood this, and knew how direct their path is, they would be spared much difficulty. I say the same equally of souls living in the world and of souls consecrated to God. If the first knew the means of merit afforded to them by their ever-recurring daily duties and the ordinary actions of their state in life; if the second could persuade themselves that the foundation of sanctity lies in those very things that they consider unimportant and even foreign to them; if both could understand that the crosses sent by Providence that they constantly find in their state in life lead them to the highest perfection by a surer and shorter path than extraordinary states or extraordinary works do, and that the true philosopher's stone is submission to the order of God, which changes into pure gold all their occupations, all their weariness, all their sufferings—how happy they would be! What consolation and what courage they would gather from this thought, that to acquire the friendship of God and all the glory of heaven, they have only to do what they are doing, suffer what they are suffering; and that what they lose and count as nothing would suffice to obtain them eminent sanctity.

O my God, that I might be the missionary of Your holy will and teach the whole world that there is nothing so easy, so simple, so within the reach of all as sanctity! If only I could make them understand that just as the good and the bad thief had the same to do and to suffer to obtain their salvation,[10] so two souls, one worldly and the other wholly interior and spiritual, have nothing more to do, one than the other. That she who sanctifies herself acquires eternal happiness by doing, in submission to the will of God, what she who is lost does through caprice; and that the latter is lost by suffering unwillingly and impatiently what she who is

---

10. See Luke 23:39–43.

saved endures with resignation. The difference, therefore, is only in the heart.

O dear souls who read this, let me repeat to you: sanctity will cost you no more. Do what you are doing; suffer what you are suffering—it is only your heart that needs to be changed. By the heart, we mean the will. This change, then, consists in willing what comes to us by the order of God. Yes, holiness of heart is a simple fiat, a simple disposition of conformity to the will of God. And what is easier? For who could not love a will so merciful and worthy of adoration? Let us love it, then, and through this love alone, all within us will become divine.

CHAPTER NINE

LOSING OURSELVES
IN GOD

All the riches of grace are the fruit of purity of heart and perfect self-abandonment.

He, therefore, who would abundantly enjoy all good has but to purify his heart, detach himself from creatures, and completely abandon himself to the will of God. In this purity of heart and self-abandonment, he will find all things.

Let others, Lord, ask You for all gifts, let them multiply their petitions; I have but one gift for which to ask, but one prayer to make: "Give me a pure heart." O blessed pure of heart! In your lively faith, you behold God within you. You see Him in all things, and you see Him at all times working within you and about you. You are in all things His subject and His instrument. He guides you in all things and leads you to all things. Frequently, you are unmindful, but He thinks for you. He asks only that you *desire* all that comes to you or may come to you by His divine order. He *understands the preparation of your heart.* In your salutary blindness, you seek in vain to discover this desire. Oh, but it is clear to Him. How great is your simplicity! Do you not know that a well-disposed heart is none other than a heart in which God dwells? Beholding His own desires in this heart, He knows it will be ever submissive to His order. At the same time, He knows that you are ignorant of what is best for you; therefore, it is His care to provide for you. He does not care that your designs are thwarted. You would go east: He leads you west. You are just at the point where the rocks are: He turns the helm and brings you safely into port. Though you know neither chart, nor route, nor winds, nor tides, your voyages are always prosperous. If pirates cross your way, an unexpected breeze bears you beyond their reach.

O goodwill! O purity of heart! Well did Jesus know your value when He placed you among the beatitudes. What greater happiness than to possess God and be possessed by Him? O state most blessed and full of charm! In it, we sleep peacefully in the bosom of Providence, sporting with the divine wisdom like a child, unheedful of our course, which is ever onward. In spite of shoals, pirates, and continual storms, we are borne on to a prosperous end.

O purity of heart! O goodwill! You are the sole foundation of all spiritual states. To you are given, and through you are made profitable, the gifts of pure faith, pure hope, pure confidence, and pure love. Upon your stem are grafted the desert flowers—I mean those graces that we rarely find blooming except in utterly detached souls, of which God takes possession as of an uninhabited dwelling, and there abides to the exclusion of all other things. You are that bountiful source from which flow all the streams that water the parterre of the bridegroom and the garden of the bride. Alas, how truly may you say to all souls, "Consider me well. I am the mother of fair love—that love that develops all that is best and takes it to itself. It is I who give birth to that sweet and salutary fear that inspires a horror of evil and makes you peacefully avoid it. It is I who ripen the sublime knowledge of God's greatness and reveal the value of the virtues that honor Him. It is I, finally, who inspire those ardent desires that, unceasingly sustained by holy confidence, stimulate you to practice virtue in the expectation of that divine object, the enjoyment of which will one day become, even as it is now (though then in a much more perfect degree), the happiness of faithful souls."

Well may you invite them all to enrich themselves from your inexhaustible treasures, for you are the source of all spiritual conditions and ways. From you they draw all their beauty, attraction, and charm. Those marvelous fruits of grace and virtue that dazzle us on all sides, and with which our devotion is nourished, are your harvests. Yours is the land of abundance and honey; your breasts distill milk, your bosom gives out the sweet odor of myrrh. Through your fingers flow, in all its purity, the divine wine that usually must be obtained by the labor of the winepress.

Let us fly then, dear souls, and plunge ourselves into that sea of love that invites us. What do we await? Why do we tarry? Let us hasten to lose ourselves in God, in His very heart, that we may inebriate ourselves with the wine of His charity; in this heart we will find the key to all heavenly treasures. Then let us proceed on our way to heaven, for there is no secret of perfection that we may not penetrate: every avenue is open to us, even to the garden, the cellar, and the vineyard of the Bridegroom.

If we would breathe the air of the fields, we have but to direct our steps there; in a word, we may come and go at will armed with this key of David, this key of knowledge, this key of the abyss that contains the hidden treasures of the divine wisdom. With it, we may also open the gates of the mystic death and descend into its sacred shades. We may go down into the depths of the sea and into the den of the lion. It is this divine key that unlocks those dark dungeons into which it thrusts souls, to withdraw them purified and sanctified. It introduces us into those blissful abodes where light and knowledge dwell, where the Bridegroom takes His repose at midday, and where He reveals to His faithful souls the secrets of His love. O divine secrets, which may not be revealed and which no mortal tongue can express! This key, dear souls, is love. All blessings wait only for love to enrich us. It gives sanctity and all its accompaniments; its right hand and its left are filled with it so that it may pour it in abundance from all sources into hearts open to divine grace.

O Divine Seed of eternity! Who can sufficiently praise You? But why seek to praise You? It is better to possess You in silence than to praise You by feeble words.

What am I saying? We must praise You, but only because You possess us. For once You possess the heart, whether we read, or write, or speak, or act, or are silent, it is all one and the same. We assume nothing; we refuse nothing. We are hermits, we are apostles; we are ill, we are well; we are simple, we are eloquent; in a word, we are what God wills we should be. The heart hears Your mandates and, as Your faithful echo, repeats them to the other faculties. In this material and spiritual combination that You deign to regard as Your kingdom, the heart governs under Your guidance. As it contains no desires uninspired by You, all objects please it under whatever form You present them. Those that nature or the evil one would substitute for Yours only fill it with disgust and horror. If You sometimes permit the heart to be surprised, it is only so that it may become wiser and more humble; but as soon as it recognizes its illusion, it returns to You with more love and binds itself to You with greater fidelity.

BOOK TWO

THE DIVINE ACTION AND THE MANNER IN WHICH IT UNCEASINGLY WORKS THE SANCTIFICATION OF SOULS

CHAPTER ONE

GOD'S INTERPRETER

The divine action is everywhere and always present, though visible only to the eye of faith.

All creatures are living in the hand of God. The senses perceive only the action of the creature, but faith sees the divine action in all things. Faith realizes that Jesus Christ lives in all things and works through all ages, that the least moment and the smallest atom contain a portion of this hidden life, this mysterious action. The instrumentality of creatures is a veil that covers the profound mysteries of the divine action. The appearance of Jesus to His apostles after His resurrection surprised them: He presented Himself to them under forms that disguised Him; and as soon as He manifested Himself, He disappeared. This same Jesus, who is always living and laboring for us, still surprises souls whose faith is not sufficiently lively to discern Him.

There is no moment when God is not present with us under the appearance of some obligation or some duty. All that is effected within us, about us, and through us involves and hides His divine action. It is veritably present, though in an invisible manner. Therefore, we do not discern it, and we recognize its workings only when it has ceased to act. If we could pierce the veil that obscures it, and if we were vigilant and attentive, God would unceasingly reveal Himself to us, and we would recognize His action in all that befell us. At every event, we would exclaim, "*Dominus est!*" (It is the Lord!),[11] and we would feel each circumstance of our life to be a special gift from Him. We would regard creatures as feeble instruments in the hands of an all-powerful workman. We would easily recognize that we lacked nothing and that God's watchful care supplied the needs of every moment. If we had faith, we would be grateful to all creatures. We would cherish them, and, in our hearts, we would thank them that, in the hand of God, they have been so serviceable to us and so favorable to the work of our perfection.

If we lived an uninterrupted life of faith, we would be in continual communion with God. We would speak with Him face-to-face. Just as the air transmits our words and thoughts, so would all that we are called to do and to suffer transmit to us the words and thoughts of God. All that came to us would be but the embodiment of His word; it would be exteriorly manifested in all things. We would find everything holy and profitable. The glory of God makes this the state of the blessed in heaven, and faith would make it ours on earth. There would be only the difference of means.

Faith is God's interpreter. Without its enlightenment, we understand nothing of the language of created things. It is a writing

---

11. In this case, the rendering in English from the Latin was included in the text of the original English translation.

in cipher in which we see nothing but confusion; it is a burning bush from the midst of which we little expect to hear God's voice. But faith reveals to us, as to Moses, the fire of divine charity burning in the midst of the bush; it gives the key to the ciphers and discovers to us in the midst of the confusion the wonders of the divine wisdom. Faith gives to the whole earth a heavenly aspect. Faith transports, enraptures the heart, and raises it above the things of this earth to converse with the blessed.

Faith is the light of time: It alone grasps the truth without seeing it. It touches what it does not feel. It sees this world as though it did not exist, beholding quite other things than those that are visible. It is the key of the treasure house, the key of the abyss, the key of the science of God. It is faith that shows the falseness of all creatures. Through it, God reveals and manifests Himself in all things. By it, all things are made divine. It lifts the veil from created things and reveals the eternal truth.

All that our eyes behold is vanity and falsehood; in God alone lies the truth of all things. How far above our illusions are the designs of God! How is it that, though continually reminded that all that passes in the world is but a shadow, a figure, a mystery of faith, we are guided by human feelings, by the natural sense of things, which, after all, is but an enigma? We foolishly fall into snares instead of lifting our eyes and rising to the principle, the source, the origin of all—where all things bear other names and other qualities; where all is supernatural, divine, and sanctifying; where all is part of the fullness of Jesus Christ; where everything forms a stone of the heavenly Jerusalem; where everything leads to this marvelous edifice and enters into it. We live by the things of sight and hearing, neglecting that light of faith that would safely guide us through the labyrinth of shadows and images through which we foolishly wander. In contrast, he who walks by faith seeks but God alone and all things from God. He lives in God, unheeding and rising above the figures of sense.

CHAPTER TWO

ENLIGHTENED BY FAITH

The divine action is all the more visible to the eye of faith when hidden under appearances most repugnant to the senses.

The soul who is enlightened by faith is far from judging created things like those who measure them by their senses and ignore the inestimable treasure they contain. He who recognizes the king in disguise treats him very differently from he who, judging by appearances alone, fails to recognize his royalty. So the soul who sees the will of God in the smallest things, and in the most desolating and fatal events, receives all with equal joy, exultation, and respect. What others fear and fly from with horror, she opens all her doors to receive with honor. The retinue is poor, the senses despise it; but the heart, under these humble appearances, discerns and does homage to the royal majesty. And the more this majesty abases itself, coming secretly with modest suite, the deeper is the love it inspires in the heart.

I have no words with which to portray the feelings of the heart when it receives this divine will in the guise of humiliation, poverty, and annihilation. Ah, how moved the beautiful heart of Mary was at the sight of that poverty of God, that annihilation, that brought Him to lodge in a manger, to repose on a handful of straw as a trembling, weeping infant! Ask the people of Bethlehem what they think of this Child. If He were in a palace with royal surroundings, they would do Him homage. But ask Mary, Joseph, the magi, and the shepherds. They will tell you that in this extreme poverty, they find that which manifests God to them more sublime and worthy of adoration. By just that which the senses lack, faith is heightened, increased, and nourished. The less there is to human eyes, the more there is to the soul. The faith that adores Jesus on Mount Tabor, which loves the will of God in extraordinary events, is not that lively faith that loves the will of God in common events and adores Jesus on the cross. For the perfection of faith is seen only when visible and material things contradict it and seek to destroy it. Through this war of the senses, faith comes out gloriously victorious.

It is not an ordinary faith but a grand and extraordinary faith that finds God equally worthy of adoration in the simplest and commonest things as in the greatest events of life.

To content oneself with the present moment is to love and adore the divine will in all that comes to us to do or to suffer through the things that successively form the duties of the present moment. Souls thus disposed adore God with redoubled ardor and respect in the greatest humiliations. Nothing hides Him from the piercing eye of their faith. The more vehemently the senses exclaim, "This is not from God!" the closer they press this bundle of myrrh from the hand of the Bridegroom. Nothing disturbs them; nothing repels them.

Mary sees the apostles fly, but she remains constant at the foot of the cross. She recognizes her Son in that face that was spat upon and bruised. These disfiguring wounds render Him only more worthy of adoration and love in the eyes of this tender mother. And the blasphemies poured forth against Him serve only to increase her profound veneration. In like manner, a life of faith is but a continual pursuit of God through all that disguises and disfigures Him—through all that, so to speak, destroys and annihilates Him. It is truly a reproduction of the life of Mary, who, from the manger to Calvary, remained constant to a God whom the world despised, persecuted, and abandoned. So faithful souls, despite a continual succession of deaths, veils, shadows, and semblances that disguise the will of God, perseveringly pursue it and love it unto death on the cross. They know that, unheeding all disguises, they must follow this holy will. For, beyond the heaviest shadows, beyond the darkest clouds, the divine Sun is shining to enlighten, enflame, and vivify those constant hearts who bless, praise, and contemplate Him from all points of this mysterious horizon.

Hasten, then, happy, faithful, untiring souls. Hasten to follow this dear Spouse who, with giant strides, traverses the heavens and from whom nothing can be hidden. He passes over the smallest blade of grass as He passes above the loftiest cedars. The grains of sand are under His feet no less than the mountains are. Wherever your foot may rest, He has passed, and you have only to follow Him faithfully to find Him wherever you go.

Oh, the ineffable peace that is ours when faith has taught us thus to see God through all creatures as through a transparent veil! Then darkness becomes light and bitter turns to sweet. Faith, manifesting all things in their true light, changes their deformity into beauty and their malice into virtue. Faith is the mother of meekness, confidence, and joy. She can feel nothing but tenderness and compassion for her enemies who so abundantly enrich her at their own expense. The more malignant the action of the creature, the more profitable God renders it to the soul. While the human instrument seeks to injure us, the divine Artisan in whose hand it lies makes use of its very malice to remove what is prejudicial to the soul.

The will of God has only consolations, graces, and treasures for submissive souls. Our confidence in it cannot be too great, nor our abandonment to it be too absolute. It always wills and effects that which contributes most to our sanctification, provided that we meanwhile yield ourselves to its divine action. Faith never doubts it. The more unbelieving, rebellious, despondent, and wavering the senses, the louder faith cries, "This is God! All is well!"

There is nothing that faith does not penetrate and overcome. It passes beyond all shadows and through the darkest clouds to reach truth; it clasps it in a firm embrace and is never parted from it.

CHAPTER THREE

HOW TO
GREET EACH MOMENT

The divine action offers us at each moment infinite blessings,
which we receive in proportion to our faith and love.

If we knew how to greet each moment as the manifestation of
the divine will, we would find in it all the heart could desire. For
what indeed is more reasonable, more perfect, more divine than
the will of God? Can its infinite value be increased by the paltry
difference of time, place, or circumstance? If you were given the
secret of finding it at all times and in all places, you would possess
a gift most precious, most worthy of your desires. What do you
seek, holy souls? Give free scope to your longings; place no limit to
your aspirations; expand your heart to the measure of the infinite.
I have that with which to satisfy it. There is no moment in which I
may not cause you to find all that you can desire.

The present moment is always filled with infinite treasures; it contains more than you are capable of receiving. Faith is the measure of these blessings: in proportion to your faith, you will receive. By love also are they measured: the more your heart loves, the more it desires; and the more it desires, the more it receives. The will of God is constantly before you as an unfathomable sea that the heart cannot exhaust. Only in proportion as the heart is expanded by faith, confidence, and love can it receive of its fullness. All created things could not fill your heart, for its capacity is greater than anything that is not God.

The mountains that frighten the eye are but atoms to the heart. The divine will is an abyss of which the present moment is the entrance. Plunge fearlessly into it, and you will find it more boundless than your desires. Offer no homage to creatures; do not adore phantoms. They can give you nothing; they can take nothing from you. The will of God alone shall be your fullness, and it shall leave no void in your soul. Adore it; go directly to it, penetrating all appearances, casting aside all impediments. The spoliation, the destruction, the death of the senses is the reign of faith. The senses adore creatures; faith adores the divine will. Wrest from the senses their idols, and they will weep like disconsolate children. But faith will triumph, for nothing can take the will of God from her. When all the senses are famished, alarmed, or despoiled, then the will of God nourishes, enriches, and fortifies faith, which smiles at these apparent losses like the commander of an impregnable fortress smiles at the futile attacks of an enemy.

When the will of God reveals itself to a soul who manifests a desire to wholly possess her, if the soul freely gives herself in return, she experiences most powerful assistance in all difficulties. She then tastes by experience the happiness of that coming of the Lord, and her enjoyment is in proportion to the degree in which she has learned to practice that self-abandonment that must bring her at all moments face-to-face with this will, which is ever worthy of adoration.

CHAPTER FOUR

MYSTERIOUS UTTERANCES

God reveals Himself to us as mysteriously, as worthy of adoration, and with as much reality in the most ordinary events as in the great events of history and the Holy Scriptures.

The written Word of God is full of mystery. His word expressed in the events of the world is no less so. These two books are truly sealed; the letter of both kills.

God is the center of faith, which is an abyss from whose depths shadows rise that encompass all that comes forth from it. God is incomprehensible; so also are His works, which require our faith. All these words, all these works, are but obscure rays, so to speak, of a sun still more obscure. In vain we strive to gaze upon this sun and its rays with the eyes of our body. The eyes of the soul itself, through which we behold God and His works, are no less closed. Obscurity here takes the place of light; knowledge is ignorance, and we see though not seeing.

Holy Scripture is the mysterious language of a still more mysterious God. The events of the world are the mysterious utterances of this same hidden and inscrutable God. They are drops of the ocean, but an ocean of shadows. Every rivulet, every drop of the stream, bears the impression of its origin. The fall of the angels, the fall of man, the wickedness and idolatry of men before and after the flood, in the time of the patriarchs who knew the history of creation, with its recent preservation, and related it to their children—these are the truly mysterious words of Holy Scripture. A handful of men preserved from idolatry amid the general corruption of the whole world until the coming of the Messiah; evil always dominant, always powerful; the little band of the defenders of the faith always ill-treated, always persecuted; the persecution of Christ; the plagues of the Apocalypse—in these behold the words of God. It is what He has revealed. It is what He has dictated. And the effects of these terrible mysteries, which endure until the end of time, are still the living words of God by which we learn His wisdom, goodness, and power. All the events in the history of the world show forth these attributes and glorify Him therein. We must believe it blindly, for, alas, we cannot see.

What does God teach us by heretics and all the enemies of His church? They preach forcibly. They all show forth His infinite perfections. So do Pharaoh and all the impious hosts who followed him and will still follow him. Though, truly, to the evidence of our senses, the end of all these is most contrary to the divine glory. We must close our corporal eyes and cease to reason if we would read the divine mysteries in all this.

Lord, You speak to all mankind by general events. All revolutions are but the tides of Your providence, which excite storms and tempests in the minds of the curious. You speak to each one in particular by the events of his every moment. But instead of respecting the mystery and obscurity of Your words, and hearing Your voice in all the occurrences of life, they see in them only chance or the acts, the caprice, of men. They find fault in everything. They would add to, diminish, reform—in fact, they indulge in liberties with these living words of God, while they would consider it a sacrilege to alter a comma of the Holy Scriptures. The Scriptures they revere: they are the word of God, they tell you; they are true and holy. Though they may comprehend them little, their veneration for them is no less great, and they justly give honor and glory to God for the depth of His wisdom.

But, dear souls, do you have no respect for the words that God addresses to you each moment—words that are not conveyed to you by means of ink and paper but by what you have to do and to suffer from moment to moment? Do these words merit nothing from you? Why do you not revere the truth and will of God in all things? There is nothing that fully satisfies you; you criticize and cavil at all that happens. Do you not see that you try to measure by the senses and reason what can be measured by faith alone? And that while reading the word of God in the Holy Scriptures with the eyes of faith, you gravely err when you read with other eyes this same word in His works?

CHAPTER FIVE

A LIVING GOSPEL

The divine action continues in our hearts the revelation begun in Holy Scripture, but the characters in which it is written will be visible only at the last day.

"*Jesus Christ,*" says the apostle, "*the same yesterday, and to day, and for ever.*"[12] From the beginning of the world, He was, as God, the principle of the life of just souls. From the first moment of His incarnation, His humanity shared this prerogative of His divinity. Throughout our entire lives, He is working within us. The time of this world is but a day, and this day is full of Him. Jesus Christ lived, and He still lives. He began in Himself, and He continues in His saints, a life that will never end. O life of Jesus that embraces and exceeds all ages! Life that unceasingly works

---

12. Hebrews 13:8.

new wonders! If the world is incapable of embracing all that could have been written of the actual life of Jesus, of all that He said and did upon the earth;[13] if the Gospels give us only a few traits of it; if so little is known even of that first hidden yet fruitful hour of Bethlehem—how many gospels would have to be written to relate all the moments of that mystic life of Jesus Christ that multiplies wonders infinitely, multiplies them eternally! For, all times, properly speaking, are but the history of the divine action.

The Holy Spirit has marked in infallible and incontestable characters certain moments of this vast duration and gathered in the Scriptures some drops of this boundless ocean. We see therein the secret and hidden ways by which He has manifested Jesus Christ to the world. We can follow the channels and veins that, amid the confusion of the children of men, distinguish this Firstborn. The Old Testament is but a small portion of the innumerable and inscrutable ways of this divine work. It contains only what is necessary to reach Jesus Christ. The Holy Spirit held the rest hidden in the treasures of His wisdom. And from out of this vast sea of the divine action, only a thread of water appears that reaches Jesus, loses itself in the Apostles, and is swallowed up in the Apocalypse. So that, by our faith alone can we learn the history of this divine action that consists in the life that Jesus Christ leads and will lead in just souls until the end of time.

To the manifestation of God's truth by word succeeded the manifestation of His charity by action. The Holy Spirit continues the work of the Savior. While He assists the church in preaching the gospel of Christ, at the same time, He Himself writes His own gospel in our hearts. Each moment, each act, of the saints is the gospel of the Holy Spirit. Holy souls are the paper; their sufferings, their actions, are the ink. By the pen of His action, the Holy Spirit writes a living gospel, but we can read it only on the last day, when it will be drawn from the press of this life and published.

---

13. See John 21:25.

Oh, the glorious history, the beautiful book, that the Holy Spirit is now writing! It is in press, holy souls, and not a day passes in which type is not set, ink is not applied, and sheets of it are not printed. But we are in the night of faith: the paper is blacker than the ink; the characters are confused; it is the language of another world; we do not understand it. We will read its gospel only in heaven. Oh, if we could only see this life of God in all creatures, in all things, and learn to regard them not in themselves but as the instruments of His will! If we could see how the divine action impels them here and there, unites them, disperses them, opposes them, and leads them by contrary ways to the same end, we would recognize that all things have their purpose, their reason, their proportion, and their relations in this divine work. But how shall we read this book, with its hidden, innumerable, contradictory, and obscure characters? If the combinations of twenty-six letters are incomprehensible to us and suffice to form an unlimited number of different volumes, each admirable of its kind, who can express what God does in His universe? Who can read and comprehend a book so vast, in which there is not a letter that does not have its own significance and does not contain in its littleness profound mysteries?

Mysteries are neither seen nor felt; they are the subjects of faith. Faith judges their worth and truth only by their source, for they are so obscure in themselves that all their external appearances serve only to conceal them and mislead those who judge by reason alone.

Teach me, O divine Spirit, to read in this book of life! I would become Your disciple and, like a little child, believe what I cannot see. It suffices that my Master speaks. He tells me this, He proclaims that. His words are arranged in one form, He interprets them in another. That suffices me. I receive all as He presents it. I do not see the reason thereof, but I know He is the infallible Truth. His words, His actions, are truth. He wills that these letters should form a word; other letters, another word. There might be only three letters, or six letters; yet no more are required, and less would mar the sense. He alone who knows all thought can combine the characters to express it. Everything is significant; everything has a perfect meaning. This line purposely ends here; there is not a comma lacking in it, nor one useless period. I believe it now, but on that glorious day, when so many mysteries will be revealed me, I will see what I now only confusedly comprehend. And that which appears so obscure, so perplexing, so contradictory to reason, so vague, and so visionary will enrapture and delight me to all eternity with the beauty, the order, the meaning, the wisdom, and the inconceivable marvels I will discover in it.

CHAPTER SIX

THIS COMMUNION OF EVERY MOMENT

Divine love is communicated to us through the veil of creatures,
as Jesus communicates Himself to us through the veil
of the eucharistic species.

What sublime truths are hidden even from Christians who believe
they are most enlightened! How many are there who realize that
every cross, every action, every attraction in the order of God gives
Him to us in a manner that cannot be better explained than by
comparison with the august mystery of the Eucharist! Yet what
is more certain? Does not reason, as well as faith, reveal to us the
real presence of divine love in all creatures, in all the events of life,
as infallibly as the word of Christ and His church reveal to us the
presence of the sacred body of the Savior under the eucharistic

species? Do we not know that the divine love seeks to communicate itself to us through all creatures and through all events? That it has effected, ordered, or permitted all our surroundings, all that befalls us, only in view of this union that is the sole end of all God's designs? That for this end He makes use of the worst as well as the best creatures, of the most grievous as well as the most pleasing events? And that our union with Him is even the more meritorious when the means that serve to make the union closer are of a nature repugnant to us?

But if all this is true, why should each moment not be a form of communion in which we receive divine love? And why should this communion of every moment not be as profitable to our souls as that in which we receive the body and blood of the Son of God? This latter, it is true, possesses sacramental grace, which the other does not. On the other hand, how much more frequently may not this first form of communion be repeated, and how greatly may its merit be increased, by the perfection of the dispositions with which it is accomplished! Therefore, how true it is that the holiest life is mysterious in its simplicity and apparent lowliness! O heavenly banquet! O never-ending feast! A God always given and always received. Not in sublime splendor or glorious light but in utter infirmity, weakness, and nothingness! What the natural man condemns and human reason rejects, God chooses and makes mysteries thereof, sacraments of love, giving Himself to souls through that which would seem to injure them most, and in proportion to their faith that finds Him in all things.

CHAPTER SEVEN

RECOGNIZING THE DIVINE WILL

The divine action, the will of God, is as unworthily treated and disregarded in its daily manifestation by many Christians as was Jesus in the flesh by the religious leaders.

What infidelity we find in the world! How unworthily men think of God! They criticize His divine action as they would not dare to criticize the work of the humblest artisan. They would force Him to act within the narrow limits of their weak reason and follow its rules. They pretend to reform all things. They unceasingly complain and murmur.

They are shocked at the treatment Jesus received at the hands of the religious leaders. Ah! Divine Love! Adorable Will! Infallible Action! How do they look upon You? Can the divine will err? Can anything it sends be amiss? "But I have this to do. I need such a thing. I have been deprived of the necessary means. That man thwarts me in such good works. Is this not most unreasonable? This sickness overtakes me when I absolutely need my health." No, dear souls, the will of God is all that is absolutely necessary for you. Therefore, you do not need what God withholds from you— you lack nothing. If you could rightly read these things that you call accidents, disappointments, misfortunes, and contradictions, which you find unreasonable and untimely, you would blush with confusion. You would regard your murmurs as blasphemies. But you do not reflect that all these things are simply the will of God. This will, so worthy of adoration, is blasphemed by His dear children who fail to recognize it.

When You were upon earth, O my Jesus, the religious leaders treated You like a sorcerer and called You a Samaritan. And now that You live in all ages, how do we regard Your will, which is forever worthy of adoration, praise, and blessing? Has there been a moment from the time of creation to this present time in which we live, and will there be one to the last day, in which the holy name of God is not worthy of praise? That name that fills all time and all the events of time, that name that renders all things salutary?

What! Can that which is called the will of God work me harm? Shall I fear, shall I fly from the will of God? Ah, where shall I go to find something more profitable if I fear the divine action and resist the effect of the divine will?

How faithfully we should listen to the words that are, each moment, uttered in the depths of our hearts! If our senses, our reason, do not hear, if they do not penetrate the truth and wisdom of these words, is it not because of their incapacity to divine eternal truths? Should I be surprised that a mystery disconcerts reason? God speaks; it is a mystery. Therefore, it is death to the senses and reason, for it is the nature of mysteries to immolate to themselves sense and reason. Through faith, mystery becomes the life of the heart. To all else, it is contradiction. The divine action kills while it quickens. The more we feel death, the firmer our faith that it will give life. The more obscure the mystery, the more light it contains. Hence it is that the simple soul finds nothing more divine than that which is least so externally. The life of faith wholly consists in this constant struggle against the senses.

CHAPTER EIGHT

LISTENING TO GOD'S VOICE

The revelation of the present moment is the more profitable that it is addressed directly to us.

We are truly instructed only by the words that God pronounces expressly for us. It is neither by books nor curious research that we become learned in the science of God. These means, in themselves, give us but a vain knowledge, which serves only to confuse us and inflate us with pride.

What really instructs us is all that comes to us by the order of God from one moment to another. This is the knowledge of experience, which Christ Himself was pleased to acquire before teaching. It was indeed the only knowledge in which, according to the words of the Gospels, He could grow. For, as God, there was no degree of speculative knowledge that He did not possess. But if this knowledge was necessary for the incarnate Word Himself, it is absolutely necessary for us if we would speak to the hearts of those whom God sends to us.

We know perfectly only what we have learned by experience through suffering and action. This is the school of the Holy Spirit, who utters the words of life to the heart. All that we say to others should come from this source. Whatever we read, whatever we see, becomes divine science only through the fruitfulness, the virtue, the light that the possession of this experience gives. Without this science, all our learning is like unleavened dough, lacking the salt and seasoning of experience. The mind is filled with crude, unfledged ideas; and we are like the dreamer who, knowing all the highways of the world, misses the path to his own home.

Therefore, we have only to listen to God's voice from moment to moment if we would learn the science of the saints, which is all practice and experience.

Do not heed what is said to others. Listen only to what is uttered for you and to you. You will find in it that which is sufficient to exercise your faith, for this hidden language of God, by its very obscurity, exercises, purifies, and increases your faith.

CHAPTER NINE

THE FOUNTAIN OF
LIVING WATERS

The revelation of the present moment is an inexhaustible
source of sanctity.

O all you who thirst, know that you do not have far to seek for the fountain of living waters. It springs close to you in the present moment. Hasten, then, to approach it. Why, with the source so near, do you weary yourselves by running after shallow streams, which only excite your thirst and give you to drink in small measure? The source alone can satisfy you; it is inexhaustible. If you would think, write, and live like the prophets, apostles, and saints, then abandon yourself, like them, to divine inspiration.

O Love too little known! Men think Your marvels are over and that we have but to copy Your ancient works and quote Your former teachings! And they do not see that Your inexhaustible action is an infinite source of new thoughts, new sufferings, new works, new patriarchs, new prophets, new apostles, and new saints who have no need to copy the life or writings one of the other but only to live in perpetual self-abandonment to Your secret operations. We are accustomed to quote "the first ages of the church— the times of the saints!" Yet is not all time the effects of the divine action, the workings of the divine will, which absorbs all moments, fills them, sanctifies them, supernaturalizes them? Has there ever been a method of self-abandonment to the divine will that is not now practicable? From the earliest ages, did the saints have other secrets of holiness than that of becoming from moment to moment what the divine action would make them? And will not this action, even to the end of time, continue to pour its grace upon those who abandon themselves to it without reserve?

Yes, eternal Love, worthy of all adoration! Love eternally fruitful and always marvelous! Will of my God, You are my book, my doctrine, my science. In You are my thoughts, my words, my deeds, my crosses. Not by consulting Your other works can I become what You would make me, but only by receiving You through all things in that one royal way of self-abandonment to Your will—that ancient way, that way of my fathers. I will think, speak, and be enlightened like them. Following in this way, I will imitate them, quote them, copy them, in all things.

CHAPTER TEN

GOD'S AMBASSADOR

*The present moment is the manifestation of the name of God
and the coming of His kingdom.*

The present moment is like an ambassador that declares the will of
God. The heart must ever answer fiat, and the soul will go steadily
on by means of all things to her center and her term—never
pausing in her course, spreading her sails to all winds. All ways,
all methods, equally further her progress toward the great, the
infinite. All things afford her equal means of sanctification. The
soul finds in the present moment the one and only essential. It is no
longer either prayer or silence, retirement or conversation, reading
or writing, reflections or cessation of thought, avoidance or seeking of spiritualities, abundance or privation, illness or health, life
or death but simply what comes to her each moment by the order

of God. In this consists that privation, abnegation, renouncement of created things—whether real or in will—in order that a soul may be nothing of herself or for herself but live wholly by the order of God, and, at His good pleasure, content herself with the duty of the present moment, as though it were the one thing in the world.

If whatever comes to a soul thus self-abandoned is her one essential, we see clearly that she lacks nothing and therefore should never complain; that if she murmurs, she lacks faith and lives by reason and the senses alone, which, failing to recognize this sufficiency of grace, are always discontented.

To bless the name of God, according to the expression of the Scriptures, is to love Him, adore Him, and recognize His holiness in all things. In fact, all things proceed from the mouth of God like words. The events of each moment are divine thoughts expressed by created objects. Thus, all things that intimate His will to us are so many names, so many words, by which He manifests His desires. This will is one in itself; it bears but one incomprehensible, ineffable name, but it is multiplied infinitely in its effects and assumes their names. To sanctify the name of God is to study, adore, and love the ineffable Being whom this name represents. It is also to study, adore, and love His blessed will at all times, in all its effects, regarding all things as so many veils, shadows, and names of this eternally holy will. It is holy in all its works, holy in all its words, holy in all its forms of manifestation, holy in all the names it bears.

It was thus that Job blessed the name of God. The holy man blessed his terrible desolation that expressed the will of God. He did not call it ruin but a name of the Lord. And, blessing it, he declared that this divine will expressed by the most terrible afflictions was ever holy, whatever form, whatever name, it bore.[14] David also blessed it at all times and in all places.[15] Therefore, it is by this

---

14. See Job 1:20–22.
15. See Psalm 34:1.

continual manifestation, this revelation of the will of God in all things, that His kingdom is within us, that His will is done upon earth as it is in heaven, that He gives us our daily bread.[16]

Abandonment to the divine will contains the substance of that incomparable prayer that Christ Himself has taught us. We repeat it vocally many times a day according to the order of God and His holy church. But we utter it in the depth of our hearts each moment that we lovingly receive or suffer whatever is ordained by this will, which is so worthy of adoration. What the lips need words and time to express, the heart effectively utters with each pulsation, and thus simple souls unceasingly bless Him in the depth of their hearts. They nevertheless sigh over their inability to praise Him as they desire. So true it is that God gives His graces and favors to such souls by the very means that seem to deprive them of these blessings. This is the secret of the divine wisdom—to impoverish the senses while it enriches the heart and to fill the heart in proportion to the aching void in the senses.

Let us then learn to recognize in the event of each moment the imprint of the will of God, of His name, so worthy of adoration. This name is infinitely holy. It is but just, therefore, to bless it and receive it as a form of sacrament that, by its own virtue, sanctifies the souls in which it finds no obstacle to its grace. Can we do other than infinitely esteem that which bears this august name? It is a divine manna that falls from heaven to continually strengthen us in grace. It is a kingdom of holiness that is established in the soul. It is the bread of angels that is given upon earth as it is in heaven. No moment can be unimportant because they all contain treasures of grace, angelic food.

Yes, Lord, let Your kingdom come to my heart to sanctify it, to nourish it, to purify it, and to render it victorious over my enemies. Precious moment! How insignificant you are to the eyes of the world but how grand to the eyes enlightened by faith! And can

---

16. See, for example, Matthew 6:9–11.

I call little that which is great in the eyes of my Father who reigns in heaven? All that comes from there is most excellent. All that descends from it bears the impression of its origin.

CHAPTER ELEVEN

THE SECRET OF UNION
WITH GOD

The divine will imparts the highest sanctity to souls; they have but to abandon themselves to its divine action.

It is only because they do not know how to profit by the divine action that so many Christians spend their lives anxiously seeking here and there for a multitude of means of sanctification. These are profitable when the divine will ordains them, but they become injurious the moment they prevent one from simply uniting one-self with the will of God. These multiplied means cannot give what we will find in the will of God—that principle of all life, which is ever present with us and which imparts to its every instrument an original and incomparable action.

Jesus has sent us a master whom we do not heed. He speaks to all hearts, and to each one he utters the word of life, the incomparable word. But we do not hear it. We want to know what he says to others, and we do not listen to what is said to us. We do not sufficiently regard things in the supernatural light that the divine action gives them. We must always receive and worthily meet the divine action with an open heart, full confidence, and generosity. For to those who thus receive it, it can work no ill. This illimitable action, which from the beginning to the end of all ages is ever the same in itself, flows on through all moments and gives itself in its immensity and its virtue to the simple soul who adores it, loves it, and solely rejoices in it.

You would be enraptured, you say, to find an occasion for sacrificing your life for God; such heroism enchants you. To lose all, to die forsaken and alone, to sacrifice oneself for others—such are the glorious deeds that enchant you. But let me, O Lord, render glory, all glory, to Your divine action! In it, I find the happiness of the martyrs, austerities, and sacrifice of self for others. This action, this will, suffices me. Whatever life or death it ordains for me, I am content. It pleases me in itself far more than all its instruments and its effects, since it permeates all things, renders them divine, and transforms them into itself. It makes heaven for me everywhere. All my moments are purely filled with the divine action. And living or dying, it is my sole contentment.

Yes, my Beloved, I will cease to prescribe Your hours or methods. You shall always be welcome. O divine action, You seem to have revealed to me Your immensity. I will but walk henceforth in the bosom of Your infinity. The tide of Your power flows today as it flowed yesterday. Your foundation is the bed of the torrent from which graces unceasingly flow. You hold the waters of it in Your hand and move them at will. No longer will I seek You within the narrow limits of a book, the life of a saint, or a sublime thought. No, these are but drops of that great ocean that embraces all creatures. The divine action inundates them all. They are but atoms that sink into this abyss. No longer will I seek this action in spiritual intercourse. No more will I beg my bread from door to door. I will depend upon no creature.

Yes, Lord, I would live to Your honor as the worthy child of a true Father—infinitely good, wise, and powerful. I would live as I believe, and since the divine action labors incessantly and by means of all things for my sanctification, I would draw my life from this great and boundless reservoir—ever present, and ever practically available. Is there a creature whose action equals that of God? And since His uncreated hand directs all that comes to me, shall I go in search of aid from creatures who are impotent, ignorant, and indifferent to me? I was dying of thirst. I ran from fountain to fountain, from stream to stream, and, behold, at hand was a source that caused a deluge; water surrounded me on all sides! Yes, everything becomes bread to nourish me, water to cleanse me, fire to purify me, a chisel to give me celestial form. Everything is an instrument of grace for my necessities. What I sought in other things seeks me incessantly and gives itself to me by means of all creatures.

O Love! Will men never see that You meet them at every step while they seek You here and there where You are not? When in the open country, what folly not to breathe its pure air, to pause and study my steps when the path is smooth before me, to thirst when the flood encompasses me, to hunger for God when I may find Him, relish Him, and receive His will through all things!

Dear souls, do you seek the secret of union with God? There is none other than to avail yourselves of all that He sends you. All things may further this union. All things perfect it, except for sin and that which is contrary to your duty. You have but to accept all that He sends and let it do its work in you.

Everything is a banner to guide you, a stay to uphold you, an easy and safe vehicle to bear you on. Everything is the hand of God. Everything is earth, air, and water to the soul. God's action is more universally present than are the elements. His grace penetrates you through all your senses, provided you but use them according to His order. For you must guard them and close them to all that is not His will. There is not an atom that, entering your frame, may not cause this divine action to penetrate to the very marrow of your bones. It is the source and origin of all things. The vital fluid that flows in your veins moves only by order of the divine will. All the variations of your system—strength or weakness, languor or vigor, life or death—are but the instruments with which the divine action effects your sanctification. Under its influence, all physical conditions become operations of grace. All your thoughts, all your emotions, whatever their apparent source, proceed from this invisible hand. No created mind or heart can teach you what this divine action will do in you. You will learn it by successive experience. Your life unceasingly flows into this incomprehensible abyss, where we have but to love and accept as best that which the present moment brings, with perfect confidence in this divine action that of itself can work only good for you.

Yes, my Beloved, all souls might attain supernatural, admirable, inconceivably sublime states if they would but submit themselves to Your divine action! Yes, if they would but yield to this divine hand, they would attain eminent sanctity. All could reach it, since it is offered to all. You have but to open your heart, and it will enter by itself. For there is no soul who does not possess in You, my God, its infinitely perfect Model, no soul in which Your divine action does not labor unceasingly to render it like unto Your image. If they were faithful, they would all live, act, and speak divinely; they need only to copy one another; the divine action would signalize each one of them through the most ordinary things.

How, O my God, can I cause Your creatures to relish what I advance? Must I, possessing a treasure capable of enriching all, see souls perish in their poverty? Must I see them die like desert plants when I point out to them the source of living waters? Come, simple souls who have no feeling of devotion whatever, no talent, not even the first elements of instruction—you who understand nothing of spiritual terms, who are filled with admiration and astonishment by the eloquence of the learned—come, and I will teach you the secret of excelling these brilliant intellects. And I will make perfection so attainable that you will find it within you, about you, and around you at every step. I will unite you to God, and He will hold you by the hand from the moment you begin to practice what I tell you. Come, not to learn the map of this spiritual country but to possess it and to walk at ease in it without fear of going astray. Come, not to study the theory of divine grace, nor to learn what it has effected in all ages and is still effecting, but to be simply the subjects of its operations. You have no need to learn and ingenuously repeat the words addressed to others. Divine grace shall utter to you alone all that you require.

CHAPTER TWELVE

THE IMPRESSION OF THE DIVINE HAND

The divine action alone can sanctify us, for it forms us after the divine Model of our perfection.

The divine action executes in time the designs of the eternal Wisdom in regard to all things. God alone can make known to each soul the design that it is destined to realize. If you were to read the will of God in regard to others, this knowledge could not direct you in anything. In the Word, in God Himself, is the design after which you should be formed and after which you are modeled by the divine action. In the Word, the divine action finds that to which every soul may be conformed. Holy Scripture contains a portion of this design, and the work of the Holy Spirit in souls completes it according to the model that the Word presents.

Is it not evident that the only secret for receiving the impression of this eternal design is to be passively submissive in His hands, and that no intellectual effort or speculation will help us to attain it? Is it not manifest that skill, intelligence, or subtlety of mind will not effect this work, but rather passive self-abandonment to the divine will, yielding ourselves like metal to the mold, like canvas to the brush, or like stone to the sculptor? It is clear that a knowledge of the divine mysteries that the will of God effects in all ages is not what renders us conformable to the design that the Word has conceived for us. No, it is the impression of the divine hand; and this imprint is not impressed in the mind through the medium of thought but upon the will through its submission to the will of God.

The wisdom of the simple soul consists in contentment with what is suitable to her, in confining herself to the sphere of her duties, and in never going beyond its boundary. She is not curious to know the secrets of the divine economy. She is content with God's will in her regard, never striving to decipher its hidden meaning by conjecture or comparison, desiring to know no more than each moment reveals, listening to the voice of the Word when it speaks in the depth of her heart, never asking what the Spouse of her soul utters to others, contenting herself with what she receives in the depth of her soul, so that, from moment to moment, all things, however insignificant or whatever their nature, sanctify her unconsciously to herself.

Thus the Beloved speaks to His spouse by the palpable effects of His action, which the spouse does not curiously study but accepts with loving gratitude. Therefore, the spirituality of this soul is simple, most solid, and interwoven with her whole being. Neither tumultuous thoughts nor words influence her conduct. For these, when not the instruments of divine grace, only inflate the mind. There are many who assign an important part to intellect in piety, yet it is of little account therein, and not infrequently prejudicial. We must make use of only that which God sends us to do and to suffer. Yet many of us leave this divine essential to occupy our minds with the historic wonders of the divine work instead of increasing these wonders by our fidelity.

The marvels of this work that gratify the curiosity of our readings serve only to disgust us with the apparently unimportant events through which, if we do not despise them, the divine love effects great things in us. Foolish creatures that we are! We admire, we bless, this divine action in its written history. Yet when it would continue to write its gospel in our hearts, we hold the paper in continual unrest, and we impede its action by our curiosity to know what it effects in us and what it effects elsewhere.

Pardon, divine Love, for I am writing about my own defects, and I have not yet learned what it is to abandon myself to Your hand. I have not yet yielded myself to the mold. I have walked through Your divine studios, and I have admired all Your works, but I have not yet learned the needful self-abandonment to receive the marks of Your pencil. At last I have found You, my dear Master, my Teacher, my Father, my dear Love! I will be Your disciple; I will learn in no other school but Yours. I return like the Prodigal hungering for Your bread. I abandon the ideas that serve only to gratify my curiosity. I will no longer seek after masters or books. No, I will use these means only as Your divine will ordains them, and then not for my gratification but to obey You by accepting all that You send me. I would confine myself solely to the duty of the present moment in order to prove my love, fulfill my obligations, and leave You free to do with me what You will.

BOOK THREE

THE PATERNAL CARE WITH WHICH GOD SURROUNDS SOULS WHOLLY ABANDONED TO HIM

CHAPTER ONE

OUR SOLE JOY AND CONTENTMENT

God Himself guides souls who wholly abandon themselves to Him.

"*Sacrificate sacrificium justitiæ et sperate in Domino*"[17]: "Sacrifice," says the prophet, "a sacrifice of justice and hope in the Lord." That is to say that the grand and solid foundation of the spiritual life is to give oneself to God to be the subject of His good pleasure in all things, interiorly as well as exteriorly, and to so utterly forget self that we regard it as a thing sold and delivered, to which we no longer have any right, so that our joy consists wholly in the good pleasure of God, and His honor and glory are our sole contentment.

---

17. This verse from the Vulgate has been translated as "*Offer up the sacrifice of justice, and trust in the Lord*" (Psalm 4:6 DRA).

This foundation laid, the soul has but to pass her life rejoicing that God is God, abandoning herself so completely to His good pleasure that she is equally content to do one thing as another, according as this good pleasure directs, never even pausing to reflect upon the disposition that is made of her by the will of God.

Self-abandonment! This, then, is the grand duty that remains to be fulfilled after one has faithfully acquitted himself of all the obligations of his state. The perfection with which this grand duty is accomplished is the measure of one's sanctity.

A holy soul is a soul who, with the aid of grace, freely abandons herself to the divine will. All that follows this pure self-abandonment is the work of God and not of man. God asks nothing more of this soul than to blindly receive all that He sends in a spirit of submission and universal indifference to the instruments of His will. The rest He determines and chooses according to His designs for the soul, as an architect arranges and selects his materials according to the edifice he would construct.

In all things, therefore, we must love God and His order. We must love it as it is presented to us without desiring more. It is for God, not for us, to determine the objects of our submission, and what He sends is best for the soul. What a grand epitome of spirituality is this maxim of pure and absolute self-abandonment to the will of God! Self-abandonment—that continual forgetfulness of self that leaves the soul free to eternally love and obey God, untroubled by those fears, reflections, regrets, and anxieties that the care of one's own perfection and salvation gives! Since God offers to take upon Himself the care of our affairs, let us once and for all abandon them to His infinite wisdom, so that we may never more be occupied with anything but Him and His interests.

Arise, then, my soul. Let us walk with uplifted head above all that is passing about us and within us, ever content with God—content with what He does with us and with what He gives us to do. Let us beware of imprudently falling prey to those numerous disquieting reflections that, like so many tangled labyrinths, entrap the mind into useless, endless wanderings. Let us avoid this snare of self-love by springing over it rather than following its interminable windings.

Onward, my soul, through weariness, sickness, dryness, infirmities of temper, weakness of mind, snares of the devil and of men—their suspicions, jealousies, evil thoughts, and prejudices! Let us soar like the eagle above all these clouds, our eyes fixed upon the Sun of Justice and its rays, which are our obligations. Doubtless, we may feel these trials. It does not depend upon us to be insensible to them. But let us remember that our life is not a life of sentiment. Let us live in this superior part of the soul where God and His will work out for us an ever-uniform, equable, immutable eternity.

In this wholly spiritual dwelling where the Uncreated, the Ineffable, the Infinite holds the soul immeasurably separated from all shadows and created atoms, perpetual calm reigns, even though the senses are the prey of tempests. We have learned to rise above the senses. Their restlessness, their disquiet, their comings and goings, and their hundred transformations disturb us no more than do the clouds that darken the sky for a moment and then disappear. We know that, in the region of the senses, all things are like the wind, without sequence or order, in continual vicissitude. God's will forms the eternal charm of the heart in the state of faith, just as in the state of glory it shall constitute its true happiness. And this glorious state of the heart will influence the whole material being that is at present prey to terrors and temptations. Under these appearances, however terrible they may be, the action of God, giving to the material being a facility wholly divine, will cause it to shine like the sun. For the faculties of the sensitive soul and those of the body are prepared here below like gold, iron, flax, and stone. And like these different substances, they will attain the purity and splendor of their form only after they have passed through many processes and suffered loss and destruction. All that we endure here below at the hand of God is intended as a preparation for our future state.

The faithful soul who knows the secret of God's ways dwells in perfect peace. And all that transpires within her, so far from alarming her, only reassures her. Intimately convinced that it is God who guides her, she accepts everything as a grace and lives wholly forgetful of self, the object upon which God labors, that she may think only of the work committed to her care. Her love unceasingly animates the courage that enables her to faithfully and carefully fulfill her obligations.

Except the sins of a self-abandoned soul, which are light, and even converted to her good by the divine will, there is nothing *distinctly manifest* in her but the action of grace. And this action is distinctly manifest in all those painful or consoling impressions by means of which the divine will unceasingly works for the soul's good. I use the term "distinctly manifest," for of all that transpires within the soul, these impressions are what it best distinguishes. To find God under all these appearances is the great art of faith. To make everything a means of uniting oneself with God is the exercise of faith.

CHAPTER TWO

ACTING BY DIVINE INSTINCT

*The more God seems to withdraw light from the soul abandoned to
His direction, the more safely He guides her.*

It is particularly in souls wholly abandoned to God that these
words of St. John are accomplished: *"You need not that any man
teach you: but as the same anointing* [unction] *teaches you of all
things…."*[18] To know what God asks of them, they have but to con-
sult this unction, to sound the heart, to heed its voice. It interprets
the will of God according to their present needs. For the divine
action disguised reveals its designs not by thoughts but by intu-
ition. It manifests them to the soul either by necessity, leaving it
but the one present course to choose; or by a first impulse, a sort

18. 1 John 2:27.

of supernatural transport that impels to action without reflection; or, finally, by a certain attraction or repulsion that, while leaving the soul perfect liberty, no less attracts it to or withdraws it from objects.

If we were to judge by appearances, it would seem most unwise to thus pursue a course so uncertain—a course of conduct in which, according to ordinary rules, we find nothing stable, uniform, or regular. It is nevertheless at bottom the highest state of virtue and one that usually is attained only after long exercise therein. The virtue of this state is virtue in all its purity; in fact, it is perfection. The soul is like a musician who unites great knowledge of music to long practice. He is so full of his art that, without any effort, all that he does therein is perfection. And if his compositions were examined, they would be found to be in perfect conformity with prescribed rules. One is convinced that he will never succeed better than when he acts without restraint, untrammeled by rules that fetter genius when too scrupulously followed; and his impromptus, like so many masterpieces, are the admiration of connoisseurs.

Thus the soul, after long exercise in the science and practice of perfection under the empire of reason and the methods with which she aids grace, insensibly forms a habit of acting in all things by divine instinct. Such a soul seems to intuitively accept as best the first duty that presents itself, without resorting to the reasoning that she formerly found necessary.

She has only to act according to circumstances, unable to do anything but abandon herself to that grace that can never mislead her. The work of a soul in this state of simplicity is nothing less than marvelous to eyes and minds divinely enlightened. Without rule, yet exactness itself; without measure, yet nothing better proportioned; without reflection, yet nothing more profound; without ingenuity, yet nothing better managed; without effort, yet nothing more efficacious; without forethought, yet nothing better fitted to unforeseen events.

The divine action frequently gives, by means of spiritual reading, knowledge that the authors never possessed. God makes use of the words and actions of others to inspire hidden truths. If He wills to enlighten us by such means, it is the part of the self-abandoned soul to accept them. And all means that become the instrument of the divine will possess an efficacy far surpassing their natural and apparent virtue.

A life of self-abandonment is characterized by mystery. It is a life that receives from God extraordinarily miraculous gifts through commonplace, fortuitous events or chance encounters, where nothing is visible to human eyes but the ordinary workings of men's minds and the natural course of the elements. Thus, the simplest sermons, the most commonplace conversations, the least elevating books become to these souls, by virtue of the will of God, sources of intelligence and wisdom. Therefore, they carefully gather the crumbs of wisdom that the worldly-wise trample underfoot. Everything is precious to them, everything enriches them, so that, while supremely indifferent to all things, they neglect or despise nothing, drawing profit from all.

When we behold God in all things and use them by His order, it is not using creatures but enjoying the divine action that transmits its gifts through these different channels. They are not of themselves sanctifying but only as instruments of the divine action that can and frequently does communicate its graces to simple souls by means apparently contrary to the end proposed. Yes, divine grace can enlighten with clay as with the most delicate material, and its instrument is always efficacious. All things are alike to it. Faith never feels any need. She does not complain of the lack of means apparently necessary to her advancement, for the divine Workman for whom she labors supplies all deficiencies by His will. This holy will is the whole virtue of all creatures.

CHAPTER THREE

THE NIGHT OF THE SOUL

The afflictions with which God visits the soul are but loving artifices at which she will one day rejoice.

Souls who walk in light sing canticles of joy; those who walk amid shadows sing anthems of woe. Let one and the other sing to the end the portion and anthem God assigns them. We must add nothing to what He has completed. There must flow every drop of this gall of divine bitterness with which He wills to inebriate them. Behold Jeremiah and Ezekiel: theirs was the language of sighs and lamentations, and their only consolation was in the continuation of their lament. He who would have dried their tears would have deprived us of the most beautiful portions of the Holy Scriptures. The Spirit who afflicts is the only one who can console. The streams of sorrow and consolation flow from the same source.

When God astonishes a soul, she must necessarily tremble; when He threatens, she cannot but fear. We have only to leave the divine operation to its own development. It bears within itself the remedy as well as the trial. Weep, dear souls; tremble, suffer disquiet and anguish. Make no effort to escape these divine terrors, these heavenly lamentations. Receive into the depth of your being the waters of that sea of bitterness that inundated the soul of Christ. Continue to sow in tears at the will of divine grace, and insensibly by the same will their source shall be dried. The clouds will dissolve, the sun will shed its light, the springtime will strew your path with flowers, and your self-abandonment will manifest to you the whole extent of the admirable variety of the divine action.

Truly, man disquiets himself in vain! All that passes within him is like a dream. One shadow follows and effaces another, just as the fancies of sleep succeed one another—some troubling, others delighting, the mind. Man is the sport of these imaginations that consume one another, and the grand awakening will show the equal emptiness of them all. It will dissipate all illusions, and he will no longer heed the perils or fortunes of this dream called life.

Lord, can it not be said that Your children sleep in Your bosom during all the night of faith, while at Your pleasure You fill their souls with an infinite number and infinite variety of experiences that are in reality but holy and mysterious reveries? In this obscure night of the soul, they are filled with veritable and awful terrors, with anguish and weariness that, on the glorious day, You will change into true and solid joys.

At their awakening, holy souls, restored to a clearer vision and fuller consciousness, will never weary of admiring the skill, the art, the invention, the loving artifices of the Bridegroom. They will comprehend how impenetrable are His ways, how surpassing comprehension are His devices, how beyond discovery are His disguises, how impossible consolation is when He wills that they should mourn. On the day of this awakening, the Jeremiahs and the Davids will see that that which wrought their most bitter pain was a subject of rejoicing to God and the angels. Wake not the spouse, worldly-wise, industrious minds filled with self-activity; leave her to sigh and tremblingly seek for the Bridegroom. True, He eludes her and disguises Himself. She sleeps, and her griefs are but as the phantoms that come with night and sleep. But do not disturb her; let the Bridegroom work upon this cherished soul and depict in her what He alone can paint or express. Leave Him to develop the result of this state. He will awaken her when it is time. Joseph causes Benjamin to weep. Servants of Joseph, do not reveal his secret to this cherished brother! The artifice of Joseph is beyond the penetration of Benjamin. He and his poor brothers are plunged into grief. They see nothing in the loving artifice of Joseph but irremediable suffering. Do not enlighten them. He will remedy all. He will reveal Himself to them, and they will admire the wisdom of He who, out of so much woe and desolation, wrought the truest joy they have ever known.[19]

---

19. See Genesis 42–45.

CHAPTER FOUR

FAITHFUL TO THE
DIVINE ACTION

*The more God seems to take from a soul wholly abandoned to Him,
the more generous He is to her.*

But let us go on in the study of the divine action and its loving artifices. What the divine action seems to take from a goodwill, it gives in *disguise*, so to speak. It never leaves a goodwill in need. For example, if we relieve the necessities of a friend with generous gifts, allowing him to know that they came from us, but later, in his interest, make a ruse of withholding our gifts while continuing to secretly assist him, the friend, not suspecting the ruse or comprehending the kindly artifice, is grieved and hurt. Bitter reflections and unkind thoughts of his benefactor torment him. But when the loving ruse is revealed to him, imagine the joy, the confusion, the love, the shame, the gratitude that overwhelm him! And are not his zeal and love for his benefactor greater from that time on? And has not the trial only strengthened his love and made it proof against any similar misunderstandings in the future?

The application is simple. The more we seem to lose with God, the more we really gain. The more He deprives us of natural aid, the more He gives us of supernatural. We loved Him a little for His gifts, but these no longer being visible, we come to love Him for Himself. It is by the apparent withdrawal of these sensible gifts and favors that He prepares us for Himself, the greatest of all gifts. Once wholly submissive to the divine action, souls should always interpret all things favorably—yes, even if it were the loss of the most excellent of spiritual directors, even if it were the distrust that they feel in spite of themselves for those who too readily offer to fill his place. For, usually the guides who, of themselves, seek the direction of souls merit a little distrust. Those who are truly animated by the Spirit of God are not ordinarily so impetuous or self-confident. They are sought, they do not offer themselves, and they never cease to distrust themselves.

Let the soul who has wholly given herself to God walk fearlessly through all these trials, letting none of them deprive her of her liberty. Provided she is faithful to the divine action, this all-powerful action will work wonders in her despite all obstacles. God and the soul are engaged in the same work, the success of which, though depending entirely on the action of the divine Workman, may nevertheless be compromised by the infidelity of the soul.

When it is well with the soul, all goes well, for that which is of God—that is, His part and action—is, so to speak, the rebound of the soul's fidelity. It is the right side of the work that, like those famous tapestries, are done stitch by stitch on the wrong side. The workman engaged thereon sees but his needle and the canvas, every little hole of which is successively filled, forming a beautiful design that is only visible, however, when every detail is completed and the right side is held up to view. But during the process of the work, all its beauty and its marvels were unseen.

And thus it is with the self-abandoned soul: It sees only God and its duty. The fulfillment of the duty of each moment is but the addition of an imperceptible point, and yet it is by means of these apparent trifles that God effects His wonders. At times, we are given a presentment of these wonders here below, but we will understand them only in the light of eternity. How full of wisdom and goodness are the ways of God! He has made all that is great, elevating, and ennobling so completely the work of His grace and action, leaving to the soul what is easy and simple to be accomplished with the aid of grace, that there is no one who cannot attain eminent sanctity by the loving fulfillment of obscure and humble duties.

CHAPTER FIVE

NEITHER TOO LITTLE
NOR TOO MUCH

*The less capable the faithful soul is of defending herself, the more
powerfully does God defend her.*

The supreme and infallible work of the divine action is always
opportunely applied to the simple soul, and she in all things wisely
corresponds to its intimate direction. She accepts all that comes
to her, all that transpires, all that she feels—all, all save sin—
sometimes consciously, sometimes unconsciously, being impelled,
not by any reason but by an indistinct impulse, to speak, to act,
or not to act.

Frequently, the occasion and the reason that determine her
course are merely of the natural order. The simple soul sees no
mystery therein but pure chance, necessity, conventionality. It is

nothing in her eyes or in those of others, and yet the divine action, which is the wisdom, the counsel, the knowledge of its friends, causes these simple things to work for their good. It appropriates them and turns them so energetically against the schemes of the faithful soul's enemies that it is impossible for them to injure her.

The divine action frees the soul from the petty, anxious schemes so necessary to human prudence. Such precautions are suitable for Herod and the Pharisees—but the magi have but to follow their star in peace, and the Babe has but to rest in His mother's arms; His enemies advance His cause more than they injure it. The more they seek to thwart and overwhelm it, the more peacefully and freely He advances. He will not court them or temporize with them to turn their attacks from Him. Their jealousies, their distrust, their persecutions are necessary to Him. Thus did Jesus live in Judea, and He still lives after this manner in simple souls, where He is generous, gentle, free, and peaceful, fearing and needing no creature but beholding them all in the hands of His Father; eager to turn them to His service, some through their criminal passions, others through their good actions, others through their obedience and submission. The divine action marvelously adjusts all these things: there is neither too little nor too much, no more good and evil than what is needful.

The order of God sends each moment the appropriate instrument for its work. And the simple soul enlightened by faith finds all things good, desiring neither more nor less than she possesses. At all times she blesses the divine hand that so carefully supplies her needs and frees her from obstacles. She receives friends and foes with equal sweetness, for it is the way of Jesus to treat the whole world as a divine instrument. We have need of no one, and yet we have need of all. The divine action renders all necessary, and we must receive all from it, accepting each thing according to its nature and quality, and corresponding to it with sweetness and humility, treating the simple with simplicity and the ungentle with gentleness, after the teaching of St. Paul and the more beautiful practice of the divine Master.

Divine grace alone can imprint that supernatural character that adapts itself so marvelously to each individual nature. It is not learned from books. It is a true spirit of prophecy and the effect of intimate revelation; it is the teaching of the Holy Spirit. To conceive it, one must have attained the highest degree of self-abandonment and the most perfect detachment from all plans and interests, however holy they may be. We must keep before our eyes the one important thing in this world—namely, the passive abandonment to the divine action that is required of us in order to devote ourselves to the duties of our state, leaving the Holy Spirit to operate interiorly, indifferent as to what He operates upon, even happy not to know it. Then, then we are safe, for all the events of the world can only work for the good of souls perfectly submissive to the divine will of God.

CHAPTER SIX

ROWING WITH THE TIDE

The soul abandoned to the will of God, so far from resisting her enemies, finds in them useful auxiliaries.

I fear my own action and that of my friends more than I do my enemies. There is no prudence equal to that of offering no resistance to one's enemies but that of simple abandonment to the will of God, nothing that so fully insures our peace. It is rowing with the tide, sailing with a wind that swiftly brings us into port. There is nothing better than simplicity with which to meet the prudence of this world. It skillfully, though unconsciously, evades its snares without even thinking of them.

Dealing with a simple soul is, in a measure, dealing with God. Who can cope with the Almighty, whose ways are inscrutable? God espouses the cause of the simple soul. She has no need to study the intrigues of her enemies, to meet their activity with equal alertness, watching all their movements. Her Spouse relieves her of all this. She confides all to Him and then rests on His breast in peace and security. The divine action inspires her with measures so just that they who sought to surprise her are themselves surprised. She benefits by all their efforts and rises by the very means with which they sought to abase her. All contradictions turn to her good. And by leaving her enemies to work their will, she draws so great and continual profit from them that all she needs to fear is that she may interfere in a work in which God wills to be the chief actor, using her enemies as His instruments, and in which the soul has no other part than to peacefully watch the working of the divine will and follow its guidance with simplicity.

The supernatural prudence of the divine Spirit, the principle of these attractions, unerringly seizes the end and intimate relations of each event, and, all unknown to the soul, so disposes them for her spiritual welfare that all that opposes itself thereto must inevitably be destroyed.

CHAPTER SEVEN

FINDING GOD AT EVERY TURN

The soul who abandons herself to God has no need to justify herself by words or actions; the divine action abundantly justifies her.

The broad, solid, firm rock upon which the faithful soul stands sheltered from tides and storms is the order of the divine will, which is ever present with us, veiled under crosses or the most ordinary duties. Behind these shadows is hidden God's hand, which sustains and upholds those who abandon themselves to Him.

The moment the soul is firmly established in this perfect self-abandonment, she is henceforth safe from the contradiction of tongues, for she ceases to have anything to do or say in her own defense. Since the work is God's, from no other source must its justification be sought. Its consequences and effects will sufficiently justify it. We have but to leave it to its own development. *"Dies diei eructat verbum."*[20]

When we are no longer guided by our own ideas, we do not need to defend ourselves by words. Our words can only represent our ideas, and where an absence of ideas is admitted, no words are needed. Of what avail are they? To give a reason for what we do? But we do not know this reason; it is hidden in the principle that animates our actions and that impresses us only in a most ineffable manner.

We must therefore leave to the results of our actions the task of justifying their principle. All is measured and sustained in this divine procession. Everything in it has a firm and solid basis, and the reason for that which precedes is manifest in the result that follows. It is no longer a life of thought, imagination, multiplied words—these no longer occupy, nourish, or sustain the soul. She no longer knows where she walks or where her path may lie in the future. She ceases to incite herself with reflections in order to bear the toils and fatigues of the route. Her strength lies in an intimate conviction of her own weakness. A way is opened to her feet; she enters and walks unhesitatingly in it with pure, straightforward, simple faith. She follows the straight path of the commandments, leaning upon God Himself, whom she finds at every turn of the way. And this God, the sole object of her life, will take her justification upon Himself and so manifest His presence that she will be avenged of her detractors.

---

20. This phrase from the Vulgate is translated into English as "Day to day utters speech." (See Psalm 18:3; this phrase is numbered as Psalm 18:2 in many Bible translations.)

CHAPTER EIGHT

PART OF A HOLY HISTORY

God gives life to the soul who is abandoned to Him, by means that apparently lead only to death.

There is a time when God wills to be the life of the soul and to work out her perfection Himself in a hidden and secret manner. Then all her own ideas, lights, efforts, researches, and reasonings become a source of illusion. And when the soul, after many sad experiences, is finally taught the uselessness of her self-activity, she finds that God has hidden and obstructed all other channels of life so that she may live in Him alone. Then, convinced of her nothingness and that her self-activity is prejudicial to her, she abandons herself completely to God and relies only upon Him. God then becomes a source of life to the soul, not by means of thoughts, revelations, or reflections (these have now become a source of illusion) but effectively by the reality of His grace hidden under the strangest appearances.

The divine operation being invisible to the soul, she receives its virtue, its substance, under circumstances that she feels will prove her ruin. There is no remedy for this obscurity. We must remain buried in it. For here, in this night of faith, God gives Himself to us, and with Himself all things. Henceforth, the soul is but a blind subject; or, rather, she may be likened to a sick man who, ignorant of the virtue of his medicines, and feeling only their bitterness, frequently imagines that they must lead to death. The exhaustion and crisis that follow them seem to justify his fears. Nevertheless, under this semblance of death, he receives health, and he continues to accept the remedies at the word of the physician.

Thus souls abandoned to God's will take no heed of their infirmities, except those of a nature sufficiently evident and grave to require care and treatment. The languor and impotence of faithful souls are but illusions and semblances that they must courageously face. God sends and permits them to exercise their faith and self-abandonment, and in these virtues lies the soul's true remedy. She must go on generously, utterly ignoring her infirmities, accepting all that comes to her to do or to suffer in the order of God, never hesitating to treat her body as we do those beasts of burden destined only to spend their lives going here and there at our will. This treatment is more efficacious than all that delicate care that only weakens the vigor of the mind. This strength of purpose has an indescribable virtue and power to sustain a feeble body; and a year of this noble and generous life is worth a century of selfish fears and care.

We must endeavor to habitually maintain an air of childlike gentleness and goodwill. Ah, what can we fear from this divine fortune? Guided, sustained, and protected by the providence of God, the whole exterior conduct of His children should be nothing less than heroic. The alarming objects that oppose their progress are nothing in themselves—they are sent only to embellish their lives by still more glorious actions. They entangle them in embarrassments of every kind, from which human prudence can see no way of escape, and, feeling its weakness, stops short, confounded. Then does the divine fortune gloriously manifest what it is for souls who wholly trust in it. It extricates them more marvelously than the writers of fiction with unrestrained imagination in the leisure and privacy of their study unravel the intrigues and perils of their imaginary heroes, bringing them invariably to a happy end. More admirably still does it guide them safely through the perils of death, the snares of demons, the terrors of temptation, the fears of hell. It elevates these souls to heaven, and they are all the real subject of those mystic histories more beautiful and curious than any ever invented by the crude imagination of man.

Then onward, my soul, through perils and fears, guided, directed, and sustained by the invisible, all-powerful, unerring hand of Divine Providence. Let us go on fearlessly in joy and peace to the end, turning obstacles into victories, remembering that it was to struggle and conquer that we enrolled ourselves under His banner. "*Exivit vincens ut vinceret,*"[21] and every step under His guidance is a victory. The book of souls lies open before the Holy Spirit, and their history is still written, for holy souls will furnish material for its pages to the end of the world. This history is but the relation of God's operations and designs upon man, and whether we shall appear in its pages and continue its narration by uniting our sufferings and actions to His divine will depends on us.

No, let nothing we have to do or suffer alarm us: It can cause us no loss. It is sent to us only so that we may furnish material for that holy history, which is increasing day by day.

---

21. This phrase from the Vulgate has been translated into English as "*He went forth conquering that he might conquer*" (Revelation 6:2 DRA).

CHAPTER NINE

THE ART OF LOVING

*Love holds the place of all things to souls who walk in the
way of abandonment.*

God, while He despoils a soul who wholly abandons herself to
Him, gives her something that takes the place of all things—of
light, of strength, of life, of wisdom. This gift is His love. Divine
love is like a supernatural instinct in these souls.

Everything in nature has that which is suited to its kind. Each
flower has its singular charm, each animal its instinct, and each
creature its perfection. And so it is in the different states of grace:
each has its special grace, and this is a recompense to everyone
whose goodwill brings him in harmony with the state in which
Providence has placed him.

A soul becomes subject to the divine action the moment good-will is formed in her heart; and this action influences her according to the degree of her self-abandonment. The art of self-abandonment is simply the art of loving; divine love grants all things to the soul who refuses Him nothing. And as God's love inspires the desires of a soul who lives for him, He can never refuse them. Therefore, can love not desire what it pleases?

The divine action considers only the goodwill of a soul. The capacity or incapacity of the other faculties neither attract nor repel it. If it finds a soul good, pure, upright, simple, and submissive, that is all it requires. It takes possession of this soul and of all her faculties and so disposes all things for her good that she finds means of sanctification in everything. What would give death to others, if it should enter this soul, would be harmless, for the antidote of her goodwill would arrest the effect of the poison. If she should stray to the brink of the abyss, the divine action would hold her back from its depths, or if she should fall, it would rescue her. And indeed the faults of these souls are but faults of frailty and scarcely perceptible. God's love knows how to turn them to her advantage and, by secret and ineffable ways, teaches her what she should say and do according to the circumstances in which she is placed.

Such souls receive, as it were, rays of divine intelligence: "*Intellectus bonus omnibus facientibus eum.*"[22] For this divine intelligence accompanies them in all their wanderings and rescues them from the snares into which their simplicity leads them. Have they committed themselves by some mistaken measure? Providence disposes a happy event that releases them. Vainly are intrigues multiplied against them. Providence overcomes all the efforts of their enemies and so confounds and bewilders them that they

---

22. This phrase from the Vulgate has been translated as "*The fear of the Lord is the beginning of wisdom*" (Psalm 110:10 DRA; this phrase is numbered as Psalm 111:10 in many Bible translations).

fall into their own snares.[23] Do they seek to surprise the soul? Providence, by means of some apparently unimportant action that she unconsciously performs, rescues her from the perplexities into which she has been led by her own uprightness and the malice of her enemies.

Oh, the exquisite wisdom of this goodwill! What prudence in its simplicity, what ingenuity in its innocence, what frankness in its mysteries, what mystery in its candor!

Behold the young Tobias: He is a mere youth, but Raphael walks at his side. And, with such a guide, he walks in safety. He feels no lack; nothing frightens him. Even the monsters he encounters furnish him with food and healing: the very creature that springs to devour him becomes his nourishment. He is occupied only with nuptials and festivities, for such is his present duty in the order of Providence. Not that he is without other cares, but they are abandoned to that divine intelligence [Raphael] charged to assist him in all things. And the result of his affairs is better than he could have made it, for everything succeeds and is crowned with prosperity. Yet his mother bitterly grieves, while his father is full of faith; but the child so sorely lamented joyfully returns to become the happiness of his family.[24]

For those souls who wholly abandon themselves to it, then, divine love is the source of all good, and an earnest desire is all that is necessary to obtain this inestimable blessing. Yes, dear souls, God asks but your heart. If you seek, you will find this treasure, this kingdom where God alone reigns.

If your heart is wholly devoted to God, within it you will find the treasure, the kingdom itself, that is the object of your desires. The moment we desire God and His will, that moment we enjoy them, and our enjoyment corresponds to the ardor of our desires.

---

23. See Proverbs 29:6; Psalm 141:10.
24. A story from the book of Tobit in which Tobias is aided on his journey by the archangel Raphael.

The earnest desire to love God is loving Him. Because we love Him, we desire to be the instruments of His action so that His love may freely operate in us and through us.

The work of the divine action is not in proportion to the capacity of a simple, holy soul but to her purity of intention. Nor does it correspond to the means she adopts, the projects she forms, the counsel she follows. The soul may err in all these things, and this often happens, but with goodwill and pure intention, she can never be misled. When God sees this good disposition, He overlooks all the rest and accepts as done what the soul would assuredly do if circumstances seconded her goodwill.

Therefore, goodwill has nothing to fear. If it falters, it can only fall under that all-powerful hand that guides and sustains it in all its wanderings. It is this divine hand that draws it toward the goal when it has wandered from it, that restores it to the path from which its feet have strayed. It is the soul's refuge in the difficulties into which the efforts of her blind faculties lead her. And the soul learns to despise these efforts in order to wholly abandon herself to the infallible guidance of this divine hand. Even the errors of these good souls lead them to self-abandonment. And never will goodwill find itself unaided, for it is a dogma of faith that *all things work for the good* of such souls.[25]

---

25. See Romans 8:28.

CHAPTER TEN

FOLLOWING THE SECRET INSPIRATIONS OF GRACE

The faithful soul finds in submission to the will of God more force and strength than the proudest of those who resist Him.

What do the most sublime intelligence and divine revelations avail if we do not love the will of God? It was through these that Lucifer perished. The work of the divine action that God revealed to him in the mystery of the incarnation excited only his envy. A simple soul, on the contrary, enlightened by faith alone, never wearies of admiring, praising, and loving the order of God, recognizing it not only in holy things but even amid the greatest confusion and disorder of events. A simple soul is more enlightened with a ray of pure faith than was Lucifer by his sublime revelations.

The science of a soul faithful to her obligations, peacefully submissive to the secret inspirations of grace, humble and gentle with all, is worth more than the profound wisdom that penetrates mysteries.

If we would learn to see only the will of God in the pride and cruelty of creatures, we would always meet them with gentleness and respect. Whatever the consequences of their disorders, they can never mar the divine order. We must see in creatures only the will of God, whose instruments they are and whose grace they communicate to us when we receive them with meekness and humility. We do not have to concern ourselves regarding their course, but rather keep steadily on in our own; and thus, with gentle firmness, we will triumph over all obstacles, even if they are as firmly rooted as cedars and as irresistible as rocks.

What can resist the force of a meek, humble, faithful soul? If we would vanquish all our adversaries, we have only to use the weapons God has placed in our hands. He has given them for our defense, and there is nothing to be feared in using them. We must not be cowardly but generous, as becomes souls chosen to do God's work. God's workings are sublime and marvelous, and never can human action, warring upon God, resist one who is united to the divine will by the practice of meekness and humility.

What was Lucifer? A beautiful spirit, more enlightened than all the others—but a beautiful spirit rebellious against God and His will. The mystery of evil is but the continuation of this rebellion in every variety of form. Lucifer, as far as lies in his power, would subvert all that God has done and ordained. Wherever he penetrates, God's work is marred. The greater one's learning, science, and understanding, the greater his danger if he does not possess that foundation of piety that consists in submission to the will of God. It is a disciplined, submissive heart that unites us to the divine action. Without it, all our goodness is but natural virtue, and ordinarily in opposition to the order of God. This all-powerful

Workman recognizes only the humble as His instruments and condemns the rebellious proud to serve in spite of themselves as the slaves of divine justice.

When I see a soul whose first object is God and submission to His will, however much she may be lacking in other things, I say, "Here is a soul with great talents for serving God." The Blessed Virgin and St. Joseph appear to have been after this model. Other gifts without this alarm me. I fear to see the action of Lucifer repeated. I am on my guard and entrench myself in my simplicity to resist the dazzling splendor of those gifts, of themselves so per- ishable and fragile.

CHAPTER ELEVEN

WHEN THE ORDINARY BECOMES EXTRAORDINARY

The soul abandoned to God learns to recognize His will even in the proud who resist Him. All creatures, whether good or evil, reveal Him to her.

The will of God is the whole life of the simple soul. She respects this will even in the evil actions by which the proud seek to abase her. The proud despise a soul in whose eyes they are nothing, for she sees only God in them and all their actions. Frequently, they mistake her humble demeanor for awe of themselves, when it is only a mark of her loving fear of God and His will that is present to her in the proud.

No, poor foolish creatures, the simple soul does not fear you. Rather, she compassionates you. It is to God whom she speaks when she seems to address you; it is with Him she treats. She regards you only as His slaves, or rather as shadows that veil Him. Therefore, the more overbearing you are, the more humble she becomes. And when you think to entrap her, you find yourselves the dupes. Your diplomacy, your violence, are to her but favors of Providence. Yes, the proud are still an enigma that the simple soul, enlightened by faith, clearly reads.

This recognition of the divine will in all that transpires at each moment, within us and about us, is the true science of the spiritual life. It is a continual revelation of truth. It is a communication with God incessantly renewed. It is the enjoyment of the Bridegroom, not covertly, secretly, in the "clefts of the rock,"[26] in the "vineyard,"[27] but openly, publicly, without fear of creatures. It is a depth of peace, joy, love, and contentment with God, whom we see, or rather behold, through faith, living and working the perfection of each event. It is the eternal paradise—now tasted, it is true, only in things incomplete and veiled in obscurity. But the Spirit of God disposes all the events of this life by the fruitful omnipresence of His action. And, on the last day, He will say, "Let there be light"[28] (*Fiat lux*), and then shall be revealed the treasures of that abyss of peace and contentment with God that each action, each cross, conceals.

When God thus gives Himself to a soul, all that is ordinary becomes extraordinary. That is why nothing appears of the great work that is going on in the soul. The way itself is so marvelous that it does not need the embellishment of marvels that do not belong to it. It is a miracle, a revelation, a continuous enjoyment of God, interrupted only by little faults. But, in itself, it is characterized by the absence of anything sensible or marvelous, while it renders marvelous all ordinary and sensible things.

26. See Song of Solomon 2:14.
27. See, for example, Song of Solomon 7:12.
28. See Genesis 1:3.

CHAPTER TWELVE

A SURE TRIUMPH

*God assures to faithful souls a glorious victory over
the powers of earth and hell.*

If the divine action is veiled here below by an exterior of weakness, it is so that the merit of faithful souls may be increased—but its triumph is no less sure. The history of the world is simply the history of the struggle maintained from the beginning by the powers of the world and hell with souls humbly submissive to the divine action. In the conflict, all the advantage seems to be on the side of the proud, yet humility is always victorious.

This world is represented to us under the form of a statue of gold, brass, iron, and clay. This mystery of iniquity, which was shown in a dream to Nebuchadnezzar,[29] is but the confused

---

29. See Daniel 2:31–35.

assemblage of all the acts, interior and exterior, of the children of darkness. These are again represented by the beast coming up out of the abyss from the beginning of all ages to make war upon the interior and spiritual man.[30] And this war still continues. The monsters succeed one another; the abyss swallows them and vomits them forth again while unceasingly emitting new and strange vapors.

The combat begun in heaven between Lucifer and St. Michael still wages. The heart of that proud and envious spirit has become an inexhaustible abyss of every kind of evil. And his only aim since the creation of the world has been to continually raise up among men new workers of iniquity to replace those swallowed up in the abyss. Lucifer is the chieftain of those who refuse obedience to the Almighty. This mystery of iniquity is but the inversion of the order of God. It is the order, or rather the disorder, of Satan. This disorder is a mystery for, beneath a fair exterior, it hides irremediable and infinite evils. All the wicked who have declared war against God, from Cain to those who now lay waste to the earth, have been seemingly great and powerful princes, famous in the world and worshipped by men. But their apparent splendor is a portion of the mystery. They are but the beasts that, one after another, rise from the abyss to subvert the order of God. Yet this order, which is another mystery, resists them with men truly powerful and great, who give the death blow to these monsters. And even as hell vomits forth new monsters, heaven raises up new heroes to battle with them. Ancient history, sacred and profane, is but the record of this war. The will of God always triumphs. His followers share His victories and reap a happy eternity. But iniquity can never protect its followers, and the deserters from God's cause reap death, eternal death.

The wicked ever believe themselves to be invincible. But oh, my God, who shall resist You! If the powers of earth and hell were

---

30. See Revelation 11:7.

ranged against one single soul, she would have nothing to fear in abandoning herself to the will of God. That apparent might and irresistible power of iniquity, that head of gold, that body of silver, brass, and iron, is but a phantom of glittering dust. A pebble over-throws it and makes it the sport of the winds.

How admirable is the work of the Holy Spirit throughout all ages! The revolutions that irresistibly carry men along with them; the brilliant heroes who are heralded with so much pomp, who shine like stars above the rest of mankind; the marvels of the age, are all but as the dream of Nebuchadnezzar, which, at his awaken-ing, fled with all its terrors.

All these things are sent only to exercise the courage of the children of God. And when the children's virtue is proved and confirmed, He permits them to overcome these monsters and con-tinues to send new warriors into the field. So that this life is a continual warfare that exercises the courage of the saints on earth and causes joy in heaven and confusion in hell.

Thus, all opposition to the will, to the order, of God serves but to render it more worthy of adoration. The servers of iniquity are the slaves of justice, and from the ruins of Babylon the divine action builds the heavenly Jerusalem.

ABOUT THE AUTHOR

Jean-Pierre de Caussade was a French Jesuit priest and writer who was influenced by St. Francis de Sales, St. John of the Cross, and Fénelon. He was born on March 7, 1675, and grew up in the town of Cahors in the southwest of France. Situated along the Lot River, Cahors was a regional hub of both commerce and administration. It was notable as a stop on the pilgrim routes to Santiago de Compostela and for its large Cathedral of Saint Etienne and stone-arch bridge Pont Valentré.

In 1693, when he was eighteen, Caussade became a Jesuit novice in Toulouse, a city with a large population about seventy miles to the south of Cahors that was, at that time, the capital of the province of Languedoc. Caussade was ordained as a priest in 1704 and, for a number of years, taught the classics and other subjects at Jesuit colleges. He later served for seven years as spiritual director to the Nuns of the Visitation in Nancy in northeastern France; he continued to write letters of instruction and guidance to the sisters even after leaving that office.

In addition to his work with the Nuns of the Visitation in Nancy, Caussade ministered in other locations and capacities. He preached for years in southern and central France, and he was a college rector in both Perpignan, in southeastern France, and Albi, located to the northeast of Toulouse. He was also the director of theological students at the Jesuit house in Toulouse. He died in Toulouse on December 8, 1751, at the age of seventy-six.

The renowned treatise attributed to Caussade, *Abandonment to Divine Providence* (titled in this edition as *The Sacredness of the Moment*), was developed from his letters and other teachings to the Nuns at Nancy. The work was not published until 1861, more than a hundred years after his death, in an edition edited by Fr. Henri Ramière; later editions also included letters of spiritual instruction that Caussade had written to the nuns. *Abandonment* has been published in many editions since that time and been translated into numerous languages.

Caussade's teachings on full abandonment to God's will and the sacredness of each moment have become a spiritual classic. The heart of his message may be captured in this excerpt from his book: "The art of self-abandonment is simply the art of loving; divine love grants all things to the soul who refuses Him nothing."